40 Excuses
to Get Together
with the Girls

Nanci Tangeman

For more information about the author and how women around
the world are using this book, visit www.nancitangeman.com.

While the author has made every effort to provide accurate
Web site addresses and other contact information at the time
of publication, neither the publisher nor the author assumes
any responsibility for errors, or for changes that occur after
publication.

ISBN: 1-4196-2879-8

Library of Congress Control Number: 2006901340

Design/Layout: Barbara Gazley

To order additional copies, please contact:
BookSurge, LLC
www.booksurge.com
1-866-308-6235
orders@booksurge.com

To my mother, Norma Tangeman,
who never needs an excuse
to get together with the girls.

Laura

I hope we never
need an 'excuse' to
get together ——enjoy.
Happy Birthday
2007

Sally x

Table of Contents

Introduction

It's 2 am and the wedding shower's ended. You and your girlfriends are saying your goodbyes, climbing into separate cars to head home to family and partners. Your stomach hurts from laughing so hard and someone says: "Let's get together again real soon – we don't need an excuse!"

You're making arrangements for the fifth family birthday party in as many months, torn between an eagerness to see your sisters, mom and sisters-in-law and a dread of another round of herding toddlers and listening to football stories from the husbands, and you wonder: "Why don't we ever get together – just us girls?"

You're looking for a parking spot while reading the last chapter of some literary magnum opus to fake it through another book club;

You're headed to another Homeowners' Association meeting because it's the only time you see your neighbors;

You're sick of "networking." You want to sit down with a glass of wine and have a good natter with the other women in your firm;

You know the women on Wisteria Lane a lot better than the women on your own block.

You need to get out more, honey. You need this book!

40 Excuses to Get Together with the Girls is for women who are game for trying something new – who are up for adventure, but don't always make the time between work, motherhood, crises or even reruns to dig out of their rut. It is for women who want to do all those things, but mostly just want an excuse to make a date with the girls. Call it "female companionship." Call it "social networking." Call it "Mom's Night Out."

40 Excuses to Get Together with the Girls gives you just that: 40 excuses to explore new areas along with your girlfriends. You choose what interests you; someone else chooses what interests her. Maybe you need to get a handle on your finances, but someone else just wants a little peace and quiet. There's something for everyone! (And everyone does not have to choose the same something!) You explore what you want, at your own pace.

40 Excuses to Get Together with the Girls gives you 40 excuses to call up a girlfriend and get together. Imagine the conversations: "The reason I'm calling is that I need to learn to mix a good Cosmopolitan." You choose the areas to explore and your friends/coworkers/neighbors/sisters-in-law choose the areas they want to explore. You all meet regularly to discuss your progress – that's your excuse to get together. Read the book; it will all make sense.

There are three kinds of "excuses" you'll find in this book:

Excuses to Play. These are activities that help us remember what we once loved to do – or introduce us to something we never had the guts (or motivation) to try: shooting photographs, bending into a new yoga pose, dancing to live music...

Excuses to Please (if only yourself). Not that the other excuses won't please you, but these will give you pleasure just by being able to utter the words, "I'm sorry, I can't, because I am required to have a manicure/pedicure/massage/bubble bath/magnum of Moet tonight. I'll get back to you."

Excuses to be Practical. These are the kinds of things that if we ever got around to doing would make our lives better, but we need a friend to give us a kick in the rear (or a martini) to get going: controlling clutter, taming finances, learning to program our cell phones...

What's your excuse? Let's get started!

How to use this book

You need three things to get the most out of this book: a group of women; a desire to get together; and the excuses in this book.

Get a **group of women** together. These women might be your daughters, your mother, your sisters or sisters-in-law, your cube-mates at work or the moms from your little girl's soccer team. Maybe there are women in your book group who really don't like to read, or fellow Bunko players who really don't like to gamble – but they love the camaraderie of girls' night out.

Whoever they are, they should be women with whom you'd like to spend more time – anywhere from three to 10 of them.

Make a commitment to each other to **get together** at least *six times* during the next three months – about once every two weeks. This sounds like a lot of time – but that's why you're here!

This book is going to give you all kinds of excuses to get together: Meet in a bar and try out new drinks for Excuse #5. Reserve a table at the hottest restaurant in town – your excuse is #17 in this case! Discuss your progress towards Excuse #20 at the park while your kids are playing baseball, or just use the book as an excuse to meet around your dining room table every few weeks to discuss how everyone else is getting on with her activities.

These get-togethers are the most important part of completing the book – and the most fun.

Now you're getting curious about those **excuses,** aren't you? There are 40 in this book and each has its own set of activities. First skim through all the excuses, and then choose up to five to complete over the next 12 weeks.

The activities are designed to stir up your life, to help you make changes (some small, some not-so-small). Try to choose a variety of topics: something fun, something useful and something wicked. Then complete the activities in the order that suits you.

As you complete your activities – or excuses – your girlfriends complete theirs. You meet every few weeks to discuss how things are going. Chances are, none of you will choose the same combination of activities, but you will all have the same excuse for getting together and motivating each other to succeed.

Remember, these are your excuses for getting together – try to choose something worth talking about!

When you get together, report your progress, but also encourage others. One week you may have figured out your net worth, but another woman may have sore muscles from a 10-mile bike ride. Another might have visited a top restaurant (without her toddler!). It's never the same twice.

And although these get-togethers are meant to inspire and motivate, as well as support, don't be surprised if a little "friendly competition" springs up. Part of the fun is seeing how different women react to the activities. Who's finished after the first week? Who's procrastinating? Who's concentrating more on getting her closets organized than spicing up the bedroom? Or vice versa?

In the end you'll find your daily life has been very different than before – very BUSY – but different. You'll have had three months of regular interaction with women who are doing interesting things – discovering things about themselves and taking the time to share the experiences.

Make the best of this opportunity. If you're already busy, choose the minimum number of areas to explore and revel in the female companionship. If you're hungry for new experiences, tackle five excuses!

Whatever you do, try something new.

Push yourself – at least a little.

Take time to relax.

Don't make excuses NOT to have fun!

Enjoy your time together.

Now let's look at those excuses!

Excuses to Play

These are activities that help us remember what we once loved to do – or introduce us to something we never had the guts to try.

1 Because Art was my first love

2 Because I love music

3 Because I live for the big screen

4 Because I want to capture the moment

5 Because I'm a mixin' vixen

6 Because I'm a wanderer

7 Because I like to win

8 Because I want to make a difference

9 Because I wanna be a biker chick

10 Because I want to know that bird's name

11 Because I'd like to walk down memory lane

12 Because I have the right (I think)

13 Because I've always wanted to write

14 Because I love the night sky

15 Because I want to try some new sports

16 Because I feel the need to create

1 Because **Art was my first love**

We all have old loves we tend to forget. Every once in awhile, though, we remember them and wonder: "What if?" Strangely enough, many of us have the same "old passion" and his name is Art. Whether you struggled with a beginner's infatuation in high school, had a brief romance in college, or keep dreaming about going back to find him, these activities are designed for all of Art's ex-lovers. (He really gets around.)

Complete at least four activities below:

❏ Visit a **gallery** or art show. Do this *three times* during the course. Go by yourself at least once. Go with someone else at least once. You can also attend an "open gallery night" in your town, but this only counts as one visit!

❏ Visit an art museum and go on a **guided tour**. This can be in your own town, on vacation or a special exhibit. Listen to the docent and see what you learn. Recorded audio guides don't count; you need to go along with someone who can answer your questions.

❏ This exercise is two-fold: First, **read a book** – nonfiction or fiction – about an artist's life. This should be a narrative, not a picture book. *Lust for Life* (van Gogh), *Girl with the Pearl Earring* or *Girl in Hyacinth Blue* (Vermeer), or if you really want to learn something, Georgio Vasari's *Lives of the Artists* (Renaissance artists). Meanwhile, as you're reading the book, spend some time with the artist's work, either with a picture book, on-line or "live" at a museum.

❏ Attend an **art lecture** at the local museum, a community center, your neighborhood gallery, or your university. Alternatively, you may go to a gallery opening or private showing at a gallery, as long as you meet and speak to the artist.

❏ Visit the **hottest exhibit** in town. Get tickets and invite a friend or two; make an afternoon or evening out of it. Go for drinks or a meal afterwards and discuss what you saw.

❏ Visit an atelier or studio and see **how art is made**. There are atelier/studio tours in most cities and some art schools have open days.

❑ Visit the **art book** section of your library or favorite bookstore and browse for one hour. Don't buy anything or check anything out; just spend time looking through different books of different art periods, different genres, etc. Do this *three times* during the course.

❑ Make a list of your five **favorite artists**. Ask three other people to list their favorites. Go to the library, a museum, the bookstore and/or on-line and view works from at least *10* of these artists (including your five) during the course time.

❑ Watch a **film** about an artist's life, fiction or nonfiction: *Pollack; Frida;* A & E's biography series on such artists as Leonardo da Vinci, Norman Rockwell, Pablo Picasso; *The Amazing Art of Beauford Delaney;* the *Artists of the Twentieth Century Series,* etc.

❑ Complete a **paint-by-number** painting "by a well-known artist." Notice how the colors are broken apart. Spend some time studying the "real thing" as you paint for comparison. (Nobody said you had to paint by the numbers! If you're so moved, paint it in your own colors.)

❑ Is there a local tourist draw that is connected to art: a well-known museum, artist's home, or pilgrimage site? Visit it. **Be a tourist.** Take a photo of yourself (better yet, sketch yourself) while you're there.

❑ Was your relationship with Art more **"physical?"** Then get moving again! Paint, sketch, sculpt, collage, shoot or weave a creation to complete this activity.

❑ Do you have a work of art that's been in your family for generations or that you picked up at a flea market years ago? For this activity, find out about a piece of art you already own – have it **appraised**, find out its provenance (history of ownership) and (because this is not an exercise designed to encourage you to sell off heirlooms) find out its special tie to your own family. If appropriate, have the piece insured.

❑ **Google an old love**, even if his name isn't Art. Go to www.google.com and enter his name "Art Smith" in the search box. Then click on the list that shows up on the screen.

2 Because I love music

When was the last time you heard live music (outside of your son's fifth-grade band concert)? Have you had the same CD in your car for six months? Do you shun anything other than pure opera/jazz/rock 'n roll? Then it's time to broaden your horizons.

Complete at least four activities from the list below:

❏ Check out the *What's On* section of your local newspaper and hand-write a list of **venues** for different genres of music (rock, orchestral, opera, house, gospel, jazz, pop, etc.) Visit at least *three* of these over the next 12 weeks. (Remember, there are often free concerts and last-minute, half-price tickets available, if cost is a factor.)

❏ **Listen** to an entire CD or album from *five* different genres, for instance, rock, orchestral, opera, house, gospel, jazz and top-10 pop. Ask friends, neighbors and family members for recommendations. You may be surprised at what they're listening to!

❏ *Every day* for a week, change the **radio station** in your car to a new music station during your commute. Avoid any stations you have pre-set – these stations should be new-to-you. (You can also complete this activity if you listen to a radio in your workplace or around your house.)

❏ If you have a (pre)**teenager,** listen to his or her favorite CD in its entirety. (If you have more than one teen, then you'll have to work harder for this activity – listen to *each* teen's favorite!)

❏ Did you know Alan Greenspan studied clarinet at Julliard? Do you have a secret musician's life, too? Do you play a **musical instrument?** If you do not play it regularly, but still have it around the house, dust if off and play it at least *three times*. If you do play regularly, challenge yourself with a new piece of music.

❏ Turn on your stereo and **sing** – while you're vacuuming, while you're driving, while you're jogging. Singing in church counts, as does singing in the shower. Do this at least *once a week* for the duration of the course. (Really belt it out!)

❏ **Read** *Inside Music* by Karl Haas (or a similar book). Karl Haas produced a radio show for over 40 years, hoping to make music more enjoyable to his listeners. Read anything designed to increase your understanding and knowledge of music for this activity.

❏ Make a **musical score** for your life. List your favorite songs from junior and senior high school, college, your first romance, your second divorce, your early-married years, your commute to your first job. Include at least *10 songs*. Now find those songs – at the library, in your closet, on the Internet – and listen to them.

❏ Give a **street musician** a donation. Do this *three times* during the program. (Don't forget to stop and listen.)

3 Because I live for the big screen

Oh, if life were only a movie! A romantic comedy, preferably. Since it's not, the next best thing is to spend a lot of time at the cinema – escaping from reality. Use these activities as an excuse to escape into whatever world you can find on the big screen.

Complete at least three of the following activities:

❏ See a **classic film** on the big screen. Whether it's *It's a Wonderful Life* or *Casablanca* or even *M*A*S*H*, try to see a film you would normally have watched on the small screen. Your local art film house can be a big help here.

❏ If it's pre-Oscar season, see all of this year's **Academy Award** nominees for Best Picture. Alternatively, view all of this year's top winners: Best Picture, Best Actress, Best Actor, Best Director.

❏ Choose your three **favorite films**. Buy or rent the DVDs and watch them with the director's comments turned on. Then watch them with the comments turned off. With features like this, who needs film school?

❏ Using a **film guide** (*The A List: The National Society of Film Critics' 100 Essential Films* is a good one) read criticism about each of the films you watch while completing these exercises. For current films, you may have to find a newspaper or magazine critic to read. Check out your library or bookstore or go on-line.

❏ Attend at least one film **by yourself**. This should allow you to concentrate on the film, not the company. Plus, it allows you to see whatever film you want – when you want to see it. (And you don't have to share the popcorn!)

❏ Whether you bicycle downtown to your local animation festival or jet off to Cannes, attend a **film festival**. Most cities have some sort of film festival during the year.

❏ Watch *three films* from a **favorites list** such as the *National Film Registry of the Library of Congress*, which includes films that are at least 10 years old and "culturally, historically or aesthetically significant." You can find this registry, along with other best-of lists at www.filmsite.org or through your library or video store. Try to watch films that you normally would not choose (silent movies, documentaries, thrillers).

❏ Read your local **film critic's** column for the duration of the course. Do you agree or disagree with him/her? Take at least *two* columns about films you have viewed and go through them, point by point, writing down your reactions to what's printed.

❏ Plan a **film review night** with your friends. Attend an early movie, then have dinner together to discuss the film. Put together questions and trivia ahead of time from reviews and previews to stimulate conversation. What are the director's and actors' other credits? Is the film a remake? An adaptation? Is it up for any awards? Is it controversial? If there's a film-themed restaurant, book a table there! (If you're on a budget, check for theatre discounts for large parties – or, plan the same evening at home with a DVD.)

❏ Choose three **different genres** of films (silent movies, documentaries, thrillers, film noir, animation, etc.) and watch one film from each. Alternatively, watch three films of the same genre, but from three different directors.

4 Because I want to capture the moment

These activities explore the more creative side of photography. For some of you, it may be a reason to return to a past passion; for others it is a way to take you beyond the point-and-shoot mentality.

Complete the first activity, plus three more:

❑ **Select a camera** to use for these activities. (This is an excellent area to explore after you've completed the activities for *Excuse #36: I want to go digital*) Learn the mechanics of this camera, using the instruction manual and/or help from a friend or professional.

❑ See how professional photographers view the world. Do *two* of the following:

- Attend a **photography exhibit** by a professional photographer. If there is a lecture or tour available, include that in your visit.

- Look at three different photographers' **books**. Read the editorial comments. Study the photos.

- Check out the winners to a **photography contest**: either local, national or international. If you cannot find a local exhibit with contest winners (this can be in a club, grade school, university), find the results of one on-line. The key is to see how different participants interpreted a specific assignment. Some good ones: www.worldpressphoto.nl (Daily Life entries); www.apogeephoto.com (Contest Archives).

❑ Make your own **photo essay**. Choose one of the following:

- Take at least four photos that tell a story or illustrate a book or poem.

- Pick a shape – triangle, square, circle – and take a series of photos that include this shape. Find the shapes in nature, architecture, etc.

- Choose a tree, building, statue, etc. and photograph it at different times during the course.

Christine: *This mother of two toddlers tackled Excuse #4. She showed her group this photo of her son, taken to complete the "boy" assignment. Would she have taken the photos if she weren't working with her friends on the book? "No," she replied. "But I would have wanted to."*

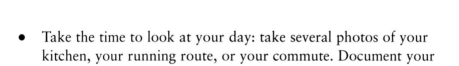

- Take the time to look at your day: take several photos of your kitchen, your running route, or your commute. Document your life. (You can come up with your own subject.)

- Photograph something that is going away: a building slated for teardown, a teen headed off to college, your husband's flat stomach, autumn leaves.

❏ Join a **photography tour** or workshop. These can range from on-location, week-long getaways to a free afternoon workshop sponsored by a local camera shop.

❏ This activity works best if you have a small, compact camera. Take your camera with you – **everywhere** – for one week. Take photos of things you normally wouldn't. Do this *two times* during the course.

❏ Choose three categories below. Hold your own **photography contest**. How will you interpret the category? Shoot several photos and interpretations for each category until you get a "winning entry." Share these photos with friends or at the next get-together.

Setting Sun	City Life	Daily Life
Tomorrow	Yesterday	Real Men
You Go, Girl	Boy	Strong Women
I	Playground	Double the Fun
No fear	Beauty	My World
Water	Still Life	Travel
Light and Form	Green	Feet
Sports	Feed Me	Outdoors
Inside Faces	Open Spaces	Forgotten
Objects	Getting Air	Postcard

❏ Take one photo that demonstrates each of the following picture-taking **tips**.

- When you're ready to shoot a photo, take three steps towards your subject. Most people stand too far back when shooting. (Don't get closer than the minimum distance recommended for your camera!)

- What is the subject of your photo? (Is it mom or her garden?) Frame your photo to emphasize the subject.

- Look your subject in the eye. Whether it's a basketball player, a child or a puppy, try to shoot at eye-level. They don't have to look right at the camera; this perspective should be enough to make a difference.

- Check out the background. A plain background is best (although a green bush usually trumps a white wall). Make sure there are no poles sticking out of heads, etc.

- Use flash outdoors, even on sunny days. This will rid your subject of shadows.

- Don't center your subject, move it to the side of your photo.

- Know your flash's range (usually 6 – 10 feet). Don't try to take flash photos of subjects too far away. Some flash functions can be adjusted to allow a longer range or to soften a harsh flash.

- Watch the light. Light is very important in photography. Try taking photos at different times of the day and in different weather. Move around your subject to achieve different lighting situations.

- Turn you camera sideways and take some vertical pictures.

- Direct your subjects. Don't be afraid to say "Everyone get closer and lean towards the camera." "Lie down on the ground and look up." "Sunglasses off/on, everyone!"

5 Because
I'm a mixin' vixen

Straight up? Full-bodied? Big, hot and now? These activities are designed to expose you to a wider world of alcohol than "whatever's on tap," and give you a real opinion about what you like to drink. Stop hemming and hawing when someone asks you which aperitif, wine or nightcap you want. Care about your booze.

Complete the first activity and four others below:

❑ Read a **magazine** devoted to wine or spirits: *Food & Wine, Wine Spectator, Wine Enthusiast, Wine & Spirits, Wine Advocate*, etc. Do this *twice* during the course. Remember, these are often available at the public library, if you want to browse back issues.

❑ Try one wine from four different **wine regions** during the course, such as Bordeaux, Stellenbosch, Napa, Champagne, Loire, the Mosel Valley, Hawkes Bay, Piedmont or Dao. As you try each wine, find the region on a map and read a little about its specialties. You can ask your local wine merchant for information, or check your wine publication.

❑ Make or order **two martinis** – one shaken and one stirred. In 25 words or less, explain aloud which you prefer and why. If you cannot describe the reason, order two more and try again, until you can properly express yourself.

❑ **Pair wines** with food. Visit a restaurant where each course is paired with an appropriate wine. Ask the sommelier, chef or waiter to explain why each wine was chosen. Listen to the answer. Enjoy the wines.

❑ **Visit** a winery, vineyard, microbrewery or distillery. Understand how wines, beers or spirits are produced.

❑ Go to a wine **tasting**; a vodka tasting; a Scotch tasting; a microbrew tasting – someplace where you can hear expert information while tasting and compare different beverages.

❑ Buy two wines from the same grape – one in a bottle and one in a box. Hold a **blind tasting** of the two. Can you taste the difference?

❑ Taste a wine or port from your own **"vintage" year** – the year you were born.

❏ Learn the meaning of *10* **terms** from the following list (www.tasting-wine.com or a good wine book can help):

Acidity	Aftertaste	Aroma	Body
Bouquet	Finish	Legs	Length
Mouthfeel	Nose	Palate	Quaffer
Acrid	Assertive	Attractive	Balanced
Big	Character	Crisp	Cutting Edge
Closed	Complete	Complex	Delicate
Dense	Depth	Developed	Elegant
Empty	Fading	Flabby	Flat
Full-Bodied	Graceful	Neutral	Pedestrian
Potent	Robust	Round	Seductive
Short	Simple	Soft	Supple
Thin	Barnyardy	Bite	Bitter
Buttery	Chewy	Corked	Dirty
Earthy	Flinty	Fruity	Grapey
Green	Heady	Herbaceous	Murky
Musty	Oaky	Oxidized	Peppery
Perfumed	Smoky	Spicy	Sweet
Tannin	Tart	Toasty	Velvety

❏ Try a **local** beer or a **local** wine. Do this *three times* during the course.

❏ Learn to **mix** *four* different drinks. At least two of these should be traditional drinks (gimlet, martini, black Russian, etc.) but two can be your own concoction. If you invent your own drink, it must have a good name and interesting back-story. Fix these for family or friends.

❏ Buy a bottle of the **cheapest wine** in the shop. Put it in a paper bag and serve it with dinner.

❏ Throw a **cocktail party**. Do it right: little black dresses, swizzle sticks, vibrant conversation and no kids.

❏ Go to **happy hour** and try whatever is on special, even if it's not something you usually drink. Or, go to a bar that specializes in a certain drink and try the house special.

❏ Throw a **kegger**. Even if it's decades since you were in college: buy a keg of beer, 100 paper cups and some cheap snacks. Charge a buck at the door.

6 Because I'm a wanderer

Do you get Slovenia and Slovakia confused? Are you constantly bombarded with country names that, as far as you remember, were not on the map when you went to school? Or are you just a closet jetsetter – someone who is always planning her next trip, at least in her mind? These activities are designed to get you to look beyond your everyday life – over the fence and out of your backyard.

Complete the first three activities, plus at least three more:

❏ Read the **international section** of your newspaper for one week. Highlight each country name mentioned. At the end of the week, handwrite a list of those countries.

❏ Choose **one country** from the list (other than your own) and do the following:

- Locate it on a map.

- Identify its leaders by name and position (Prime Minister, President, King, etc.)

- Explain its system of government. You hear a lot in the news about "fighting for democracy." How does that relate to this country?

- When was this country founded?

- What is its population? Major languages?

- Is it a part of any alliance: NATO, European Union, ASEAN?

- Handwrite this information so that you remember it. No cutting or pasting on the computer!

❏ Continue to read the international section of the newspaper and **track news** for that country for the remainder of the course.

❑ Pretend you're a **businessperson** headed to this country. What are three things you should know about doing business there in terms of business etiquette, regulations or traditions?

❑ If you were to visit your chosen country, would you need a **visa**? If a citizen of that country were to visit your country, would a visa be required?

❑ **Plan a trip** to the country. Which airlines fly there and what route would you need to take? What are three major attractions you'd like to visit?

❑ Find a local restaurant specializing in the **cuisine** of this country. Have a meal there. Or, cook a meal in the cuisine of this country.

❑ Are there are any **local festivals** commemorating this country in your town? A store specializing in foods and goods? If so, visit it.

❑ **Meet a person** from this country and make a friend. Ask questions about life there and how it differs from life in your town. Find out if what you've been reading in the newspapers is true!

❑ Apply for a **passport**. Really do it. Get the photos taken; fill out the application; send in the money and wait by the mailbox!

❑ **Visit** the country. Why not? Here's your excuse!

7 Because I like to win

How is your competitive spirit? Is it wasted on the workplace? Or has it gone latent for a few years, hidden somewhere under the sofa pillows or behind the TV set? Have you traded in the *Candylands* and *Chutes and Ladders* of your youth for hours of *Free Cell*, alone with your computer screen?

These activities will bring you good, healthy competition, while forcing you to interact with other human beings! It can mean some quality time with family, or some raucous evenings with friends. Either way, break out the popcorn and the root beer, clear off the dining room table and prepare to play to the death.

Complete the first two activities and two more:

❑ Obtain **three games** to play over the 12-week course. These can come from the toy store, your friends, eBay or even your closets. Make sure they are games that will hold your interest. Don't forget games like *Charades* and *Authors* that don't require special equipment. At least one of these games should be new to you.

❑ Schedule a time to **play each game.** This should be spread out over three different occasions. Maybe you'll want to stage one night of games with your family, a game of *Charades* after dinner, or even a quiet night of strip cribbage with your partner.

❑ Learn a **new game.** Always wanted to play chess? Poker? Mah Jongg? Have a friend teach you, go to a local games night at the community center, or take a lesson.

❑ List all the games you can remember from your childhood. Which were your **favorites**?

❑ Go to **Bingo** night at a local business or church.

❑ Take a trip to the **toy store** (by yourself) and look at the games section. Take time to read the descriptions. Concentrate on the "age 16 to adult" section if you've spent the past few years playing with toddlers. Peruse the children's section if you haven't.

❏ Gather all the games you have around the house. Choose which to keep and which to discard. Donate the discards to a shelter or other good cause or sell them on eBay or at a garage sale. Dust the others off and **play** each of them at least once, then store them in a place where they're organized and accessible.

❏ **Invite friends** over specifically to play a game – Poker Night, Bridge Night, Mah Jongg Morning.

❏ Try to remember three **drinking games** from college. If you can't remember, ask some college students to suggest three. Play *two* of the games.

8 Because I want to make a difference

"Somebody should really do something about that." These activities let you be somebody! Here is the extra push you need to get involved in your community. These activities are designed to make you ask, "What is important to me?" and "How can I help?"

Do the first four activities, plus two more:

❏ List *10* causes that mean something to you. Include political, educational, health and religious **causes**. Be specific. Not "schools," but "the number of opportunities for arts education in elementary schools." Not "healthcare," but "language skills keeping immigrant families out of well-baby programs." What areas need help in your community? What's not working right? What is working right that you support?

❏ List *20* things that **you have to offer**. These can include *specific skills*: photography, promotions, writing, accounting, word processing or *specific tangibles*: money, extra furniture, five hours per week or even *specific intangibles*: a good ear, great organizational skills, patience, a willingness to try anything.

❏ List *10* specific **volunteer opportunities** in your town. You can find these through individual organizations, classified ads, on-line (Google search: yourtown, "volunteer opportunities") church groups, friends, schools, your company. Make a list of the details for each specific opportunity:

- Organization

- Duties

- Commitment: Hours, length of commitment, monetary outlay

- Qualifications or training required

- Location

❏ Keeping in mind the first two lists you made, choose and complete *at least one* **volunteer activity** from your list that suits your availability and interests: manning the sign-up booth at a fundraiser golf tournament; running and exercising shelter dogs every two weeks; delivering meals for Meals on Wheels once a month; volunteering in a church office every Tuesday morning.

- List *10* organizations that need **cash** donations. Research how the money is spent and whether you can direct a contribution to a specific use. Make a donation. Does your employer match your donation? If so, double your donation by filling in the right paperwork.

- Start your own charitable **foundation.** If there is a need that you feel strongly about and it's not being fulfilled in your community, there may be a way for you to channel your own resources (time, talent, dollars) towards correcting that situation. It doesn't take millions of dollars (but, hey, if you have millions to spend…), just a good idea, some seed money and dedication.

- Organize and fulfill one **group volunteer activity.** This could include a teddy bear drive at work; heading a team for Habitat for Humanity; sponsoring a family for a holiday. The group could be your family, your coworkers, your friends or your neighbors…

- What do you have in your house that you're not using that someone else could? This is not an excuse to clear out old junk, but if you have an extra crib in the basement or an extra set of household appliances after a new marriage, find a recipient and **donate.**

- Ask that friends and family make a donation to a charitable cause this year in lieu of your birthday or holiday **gifts.** Or, make a donation in lieu of buying gifts for someone who would understand.

- Register as an **organ donor** (and tell your family about it).

- Attend a **fundraiser** for a cause you believe in. If there is an auction at the event – bid high. If there is a raffle – buy a ticket. If that's too easy, organize an entire table at the event and fill it with your friends.

- Are you a member of a club or professional organization? Become an **active member,** if you're not already. Volunteer to help out – plan an outing, host an event, submit an article to the newsletter, find a speaker, man a table. Support your own organizations, as well as others.

9 Because

I wanna be a biker chick

Let's face it: we all have a little leather and grease inside us. These activities are designed to put it to use – on your bicycle and on your body. Think Lance Armstrong meets Olivia Newton John in *Grease* ("I got chills … they're multiplying!") and you've got an idea of what's involved.

Complete the first three activities and at least two other activities below:

❑ Outfit your bicycle to **meet the requirements** of your state, country or county. Do you need a bicycle helmet, working headlight, rear reflector, warning bell? Purchase and install them!

❑ Learn the bicycle rules of the road. Demonstrate hand signals for turning right and left and slowing down. Know who has the right of way, etc.

❑ Plan and complete *four* different **bicycle rides** of at least 10 miles/16 km each. These should be outings for pleasure. Try to ride somewhere scenic or plan a picnic or family day-out around the rides. Tour the local wineries; meet friends before or after work for an alternative to drinks or lunch.

❑ If you have never learned to ride a bike, show that you can follow a winding course for 60 feet doing sharp left and right turns, a U-turn and an emergency stop. Complete a **one-mile bicycle ride**. (You can also use this activity to satisfy the requirements for *Excuse #37: Because I really, really need to do this.*)

❑ **Change a tire** on a bicycle. (This does not mean dropping your bike off at the corner bicycle shop!)

❑ Keep your cycle **safe**. Buy and use an approved bike lock. Register your bicycle's serial number with the police or have your name/zip code engraved on the frame.

❑ Find a friend and ride a **bicycle built for two**. Spend time on the driver's seat, as well as on the back seat.

❑ **Commute** on your bicycle. Ride your bike to work, to run errands or to a friend's house in place of your car or public transportation. Do this *four times* during the course.

❏ If you're going on a holiday, work a **guided bike tour** into your schedule. Better yet, do it in your hometown!

❏ Ride a **motorcycle**. Ask a friend who's an avid biker to take you for a ride, or go on a beginner's course for a day. (If you're a lapsing motorcycle mama who hasn't ridden for awhile, you can still hit the roads and count this towards your excuse!)

❏ Go to a **bike race**. It doesn't have to be the Tour de France (but why not?) it could just be an event at your local velodrome.

❏ Try a **new kind** of biking: mountain biking, road racing, etc.

❏ Attend a **bike camp** – whether for roads or mountains or even velodrome racing!

❏ Go from "cyclist" to "**biker chick**." Visit an appropriate store and try on the whole get-up: black leather pants, form-fitting black tee shirt, black boots. Practice your sultriest look in the mirror. Dance around the dressing room. If you like your new look, take it all home. If you don't, just take a picture.

10 Because I want to know that bird's name

If the first robin of spring landed on your windowsill, would you recognize it? Is somebody squawking incessantly outside your office (other than your boss) that you would like to curse – if only you knew its name? These activities are for those of you who want to know a little more about the visitors in your backyard – at least the feathered ones!

Complete the first activity, plus three more:

❏ **Get outfitted** like a birder.

- Obtain a good field guide. Some recommendations for beginning "birders" include: *Peterson Field Guide to Eastern Birds or Peterson Field Guide to Western Birds*. There is also a Peterson *First Guide: Birds*, designed for (but not limited to) children that lists only 188 birds. Another good one is *All the Backyard Birds* by Jack Griggs. The newest editions have color photos and excellent graphics. They are usually available at your local library. Read the introduction (especially anything aimed at first-time birders) and become familiar with its organization – by silhouette, beak type, etc.

- Even for birding in your backyard, you'll need a binocular – but unless you have a very large backyard, you won't need to spend a thousand dollars! (Easy to do if you go for the very best.) Birding books and Web sites can recommend good brands. Check eBay or borrow a pair to see if you enjoy the activity before making a large investment.

❏ Read a bird **magazine** for three months running. These are usually available at your library or newsstand. Some good ones include:
Birder's World (www.birdersworld.com)
Wildbird (www.wildbirdmagazine.com)
Birding (www.americanbirding.org)
Birdwatcher's Digest (www.birdwatchersdigest.com)

❏ Participate in a **birding trip** or tour. Local bird trips are sometimes advertised in the newspapers or through your local "Rare Bird Alert" hotline (numbers for each state are listed on most birding Web sites).

❑ **Record** your bird sightings. There are bird lists available on the Web (www.birding.com) and through your library. Print out a list and keep track of the birds you spot during the course. (You can do the same if you go on vacation, as well.)

❑ List **five birds** found in your backyard (or neighborhood). Using your field guide, write down each bird's characteristics: feeding habits, habitat, voice, range, etc. Be able to identify them by sight.

❑ Be able to **identify five birds by call** only. There are several ways to do this. First of all, you can listen to a real, live bird and imitate it. Or, you can use a cassette, DVD or Web site (most of the Web sites listed here include birdcalls) to help you. Demonstrate this – to your friends, to your boss, to your cat.

❑ Set up a **feeding station** in your garden – this can be an artsy birdfeeder, a hummingbird feeder or just a flat board with drainage. You can even get your backyard classified as a Backyard Wildlife Habitat (www.nwf.org). There is more information on making your garden bird-friendly at your library, in the birding magazines or on www.audubon.org. For this activity, however, you need only set up a feeding station!

❑ Set up a **birdbath** and put it in an appropriate place, taking into consideration predators (the family cat) and hygiene. Again, get advice from a birding magazine, Web site or local bird supply store.

❑ Participate in the annual **Great Backyard Bird Count.** On one specific winter weekend, over 40,000 bird enthusiasts of all ages and skill levels count the number and kinds of birds they see and report them over the Internet. The event was developed and is managed by the Cornell Lab of Ornithology and the National Audubon Society. For more information and this year's date, check www.birdsource.org/gbbc.

11 Because I'd like to walk down memory lane

Would you like to share your memories with others – or just preserve them for your own old age reminiscing? Here's your excuse to do something with those photos and other paraphernalia that are stacking up around your home.

Complete at least four activities:

❑ Choose **10 photos** that are rotting away in a drawer, album, shoebox, closet or stack of junk somewhere in your house. Your theme for this set of 10 photos can be anything: our family; great shots; people you miss; pets; sporting moments; places I've been; childhood; old family photos; marriage – year one; best of this year; everybody is having a good hair day; nobody is having a good hair day (except me); etc. Frame or otherwise display these photos in your home or office. You can tie them together with matching frames; put them on a magnetic or cork board; drop them into a collage frame. The key is to get those memories out there where you can enjoy them every day! (How about decorating a wall in your guest bathroom?)

❑ Choose one trip and commit it to a **scrapbook.** If it's a short trip, get a scrapbook where you can add pages. If it's a big one, devote an entire book to it. The key is – start with something you can finish. It doesn't have to be elaborate: at a minimum, mount and label the photos. You must FINISH this project to count it as an activity.

❑ **Give someone a memory.** This might be a framed photo; an old postcard you received from a friend when you were kids; a souvenir from a place you visited with your parents; a favorite keepsake with a special memory for a relative; an album of photos of your late parents for your sibling – whatever it is, the gift is the memory. Don't worry about monetary value. Or, you could exchange a memory in this way – put a note inside your gift and say "How about a copy of that photo of us when we were _____." (Try not to make it sound like blackmail.)

❑ Do you have shells and rocks and pinecones and other natural items that you have picked up on beach walks, hikes, etc.? Commit these to one central spot. This could be shelf or windowsill where you can fondle the items on demand, or it could be a pretty bowl or vase in your living room where the items are displayed for all to see. The goal of this exercise is to **honor the items** that caught your eye in the first place and remember the times when you picked them up.

❑ Make **packrat art**. Do you collect anything? (Everything?) Make some memorable art with it. Scan your children's schoolwork and make transfers for a quilt; arrange your matchboxes in a shadow box; make a collage from old post cards. (You can do this in conjunction with *Excuse #35: Because I want to see the back of my closet*, but remember to make it memory-driven.)

❑ Think of **12-20 questions** you'd like to ask somebody – your spouse, your son, your parent, a friend, your grandparent, etc. These could be questions about childhood life or when they were in the Army or their everyday life or something more psychological – just make sure the questions are interesting for both of you. Package them in a clever way – fold them, wrap them as scrolls, etc. Give this package to the person who has the answers. Make a date each month to have the person pull a question out of the package and talk about the answer with you. (Make these fun questions, or you'll never get past the first month!) The extra questions are so the person may "pass" on a question. Use this as a gift or a way to share memories between generations. If it's an elderly relative, you may want to record the answers.

❑ Do you have **favorite recipes** that have been handed down from generation to generation? Capture them in a cookbook. Include photos of the cooks and make copies for the wannabe chefs in your family.

❑ **Capture a time** of your life in a box. Not everything has to be committed to a time-consuming scrapbook or photo album. Buy and/or decorate a pretty box and put memorabilia inside from a specific time in your life: high school; your marriage; the year after your divorce; your backpacking trip through Europe…

❏ Make an **audio memory**. Record a sound that you might otherwise lose: your child's singing; your grandmother's stories; your partner's garage band ... You could also do this on video, but focus on the sound.

❏ Are you wishing you had more memories to remember? Commit to **making a family holiday more memorable** this year. Bring back a tradition or start a new one. It could be as simple as a round robin question at the dinner table: "What are you thankful for?" at Thanksgiving; "What's your first childhood memory?" at a birthday party. Or it might be bringing back a favorite childhood dish or turning off the Internet and the TV on Christmas Day.

❏ Remember when you could drop your film off at the little blue Fotomat building and later, when you came back, the Foto-mate would have 12, 24 or 36 pictures ready for you to take home? For this exercise, get **36 photos** printed from your digital camera or your computer – and share them with somebody! Don't hide your memories on your hard drive! (Do this in conjunction with *Excuse #36: Because I want to go digital.*)

❏ Make a **shadow box** of an event or era. Include the ticket stubs you have at the bottom of your drawer; or the badge from your last job before retirement along with your first pay stub. Anything that gives you a fond memory is worthy. Think of it as a little shrine to a part of your life.

❏ Organize **your children's class work** into files. Create an accordion file for each child. Deposit memorabilia from each school year into the file. When they move out of the house, you decide: keep it or pack it along with them?

❏ Frame a **child's work of art** and display it.

❏ Attend a **memory art class,** but only purchase what you will use immediately – supplies for one shadow box or scrapbook or memory box. Better yet, attend a class where you leave with your finished project.

❑ Set aside one hour. Read old love letters; page through your high school yearbooks; look at your family photo albums; pick an old journal and read it; go through a checkbook register that's at least a decade old – do anything that causes you to take a short walk down memory lane. Alternatively, ask to see a friend's photo album or high school yearbook (but not her checkbook register) and listen to her stories. This is your excuse to **relax, remember, and enjoy**. Do this *three times* during the program.

❑ Don't lose your memory! Gather your important negatives and put them in a **fireproof safe** or safe deposit box. This is especially important for old family photos and wedding photos. Back up your digital photos (onto CD) and store them with the negatives, as well.

❑ Keep a **journal** for the remainder of this program. This can be a daily or weekly journal; you can do it on your computer or hand-write it in a pretty book, but commit to a schedule and keep it for the next three months, or so.

❑ Edit a video. Produce a **highlights** reel of your vacation or your child's play. This will make it less painful (I mean, *more enjoyable*) for friends and family to watch. You can also edit a slide show to complete this exercise. It can be done on-line or presented on a television or projection screen for viewing.

❑ **Go digital** with your memories. For the tech savvy (or not) convert your analog memories into digital ones. This includes having old negatives or photos scanned; having audio or videocassettes trans-ferred to DVD or CD; even old family movies can be converted. This makes these memories much more accessible and allows you to share them easily – often over the Internet! What a great excuse to take another look! Choose at least one reel, cassette or set of photos to convert to complete this exercise. (This makes a great birthday or anniversary gift!)

❑ Have a **painting or photograph** made of your family, yourself or even your pet. Display it prominently (even if you or your dog is naked).

12 Because I have the right (I think)

How much information did you retain from your high school Social Studies class? Don't you wish you could recall some of it when you hear a news story that makes your blood boil, or you want to change something in your town? "What about our Constitutional rights?" you want to shout, but then you can't remember if you truly do have that particular right in the Constitution. Here's an excuse to review those basics you may have forgotten. See how you react to learning a few of them now that you've a little experience under your belt.

Complete the first activity, plus three more:

❏ **Register to vote.** You can find out how at your local town hall, library or on-line at www.eac.gov/register_vote.asp or www.overseasvotefoundation.org (overseas voting). Remember, when the US was born, only white men with property were allowed to vote. African Americans, women, Native Americans, non-English speakers and citizens between the ages of 18 and 21 all had to fight for the right. Are you using your right? Your first step is to register.

❏ **Vote.** All of the above applies here. If there is an election held during your course, participate. With the right to vote comes the responsibility to be informed. Read your voter's pamphlet and gather information from more than one source in order to hear different points of view.

❏ Learn the names, party affiliations and platforms of **your representatives.** When does each come up for reelection? Learn how they voted on at least one issue. There are several sources for this: your library, on-line at www.senate.gov, www.vote-smart.org and www.congress.org, and through your local government. (Again, know where your information about candidates originates and try to get more than one point of view on where they stand.)

❏ Work on a **campaign** for a person or cause you believe in. Is there something in your town or state that is threatened or needs to be changed or protected? Then get involved. Don't wait for somebody else to do it. Apply your professional skills (accounting, promotions, computer, public speaking) or your energy (answering phones, canvassing neighborhoods) to work towards change.

❏ Read the ***Constitution of the United States.*** What amendments have been made during your lifetime? A good source for this information is the National Archives Web site www.archives.gov. There is a transcript of the original version with hyperlinks to changes, as well as a printer-friendly version. (Use the subject index on the site.) Better yet, borrow your sixth-grader's history textbook!

❏ Memorize the ***Bill of Rights.*** You remember those – the first 10 amendments to the *Constitution of the United States.* You don't have to be able to recite them word-for-word, but be able to discuss the rights you have under each amendment.

❏ Choose an issue that is important to you. Write a **letter** to your representative – local, state or federal. Express your feelings and be sure to mention that you are registered to vote in his/her district. Your state's Web site or your library will have tips/ addresses for contacting representatives.

❏ Watch three good **political films** for inspiration – from *All the President's Men* to *Z.* Have some laughs with *Dave.* Relive one rendition of history with *JFK.* Sample another country's story with *Cry Freedom.* Get a political crush with *The American President.*

❏ Read a **political book** – anything new and "insider" will do. Try to read something that goes against your beliefs. Did it infuriate you? Did it change your point of view at all?

13 Because I've always wanted to write

Writing is one of those wonderful activities that's cheap, portable and personal. Everybody's writing is different – one woman knows she has a novel inside; another just wants to record her child's childhood. Whether it's fiction, non-fiction (or a little bit of both) these activities are designed to get the pen on the page and the thoughts out of your head.

Complete five or more of the following activities:

❏ **Write freely.** Free writing frees your mind and transfers your thoughts to the page. There are many guidelines for free writing, including these by writing guru Natalie Goldberg (www.nataliegoldberg.com). Free write for 10 minutes, *once a week*, during the course. What do you write about? Write about the first thing that pops into your mind. Do not use a computer, use a pen.

- Once you start writing, don't stop for the allotted 10 minutes.

- Keep your hand moving. Don't pause to reread the line.

- Don't cross out. Even if you write something you didn't mean to write, leave it.

- Don't worry about spelling or grammar or punctuation.

- Lose control.

- Don't think. Don't get logical.

- Go for the jugular. If something comes up in your writing that is scary or naked, dive right into it.

❏ **Go somewhere** and write. It doesn't have to be a French bistro and you don't have to wear a beret, but you are guaranteed to feel at least a tiny bit exotic. Describe the place where you are: the people, the activities. Don't just write about colors or textures, write about how you feel about things: Does the air conditioning irritate you? Does that man across the room give you the creeps? Why? Do this exercise *three* times in *three* different locations.

❏ Write an **Op-Ed piece** or a letter to the editor. Is there something you feel strongly about? Something you need to get off your chest? You don't necessarily have to send the piece, but writing down and organizing your argument can be invigorating.

❏ **Handwrite** a letter to someone to whom you normally would send an email. Use special writing paper – give it a squirt of cologne. See how your message differs when you write something down on a page. How do you organize your thoughts without cut, paste and spell-check? Does it seem like a special occasion? Be sure to find out how the recipient feels.

❏ Write a **love letter.** Pour your thoughts onto the page. Be romantic. Be naughty. Be sensuous. Describe your feelings when you're together – describe your feelings when you're apart. Now, do you have the guts to send it?

❏ This is an addictive exercise, so be careful. Anyone familiar with creativity motivator Julia Cameron (www.theartistsway.com) will have tried this. Write what Cameron calls **"Morning Pages."** As soon as you wake up in the morning, before you even start the coffee pot, write three pages of longhand. Write whatever comes into your mind. Do you feel fat? How did you sleep? Is the sun shining through your window just right? The pages don't have to make sense. Maybe you are writing about how you have nothing to write? Or you need cat litter. Whine. Be petty. Be boring. Be cheerful. You will never show them to anybody else, so don't worry about how you sound. Do this *every day* of the course. Keep an eye out for any "shifts in consciousness."

❏ Set aside one hour for this exercise. Write about the place **where you grew up.** Try not to be sentimental. Fill in details of how things looked, tasted, sounded. Try to write from different points of view: your own, your dog's, a visiting relative. Think about place names that just roll off your tongue. (What does the Space Needle have to do with space?) Remember – write down the details!

❏ **Market knowledge.** This exercise is especially good if you are hoping to submit an article or story "someplace," but just don't know how or where. Get a copy of the latest *Writer's Market* (www.writersmarket.com). This reference book has over 1,000 places that buy writing – magazines, journals, publishers, script buyers – plus agents' listings. Make a list of *10* things you know about or like to write about. Then use the book to find *three* potential markets for each item on your list. For instance, if you are an expert on making scrapbooks, check out the Hobby and Crafts publications. Read each description, along with submission guidelines and payment details. Then, armed with your list of potential markets, go to your library or bookstore and see examples of each publication. After completing this exercise, you should have a more realistic idea of the marketplace for your writing.

❏ You love to write, but you can never think of **something to write about!** For this exercise you will need about one hour. For the first 10 minutes, make a list of topics you might like to write about. These can be far ranging, from America's history to your grandmother's Plymouth to the meeting you had at work. Just make a numbered list. After 10 minutes, choose one thing on the list and write for another 10 minutes. Do this four more times (to fill in the hour). Do this *three* times (with new topic lists) during the course to complete this activity. At the end of the three sessions you should realize how many interesting topics you have to write about.

❏ This writing exercise doesn't even involve writing! For this exercise (also from Goldberg), you will need a time-frame (at least 20 minutes long) when you can talk, **out loud,** to yourself: your commute, your run, your vacuuming session, your lunch break (be sure to hold a cell phone up to your ear). Start by saying "I remember ..." then just keep talking. It doesn't have to flow well or be coherent. Just let your thoughts out into the universe. There's no pressure to edit; no pressure to preserve them. Just ramble on and on and see where it leads you. Do this *three* times during the course. You can use different beginnings ("I know" or "I see") and, if you'd like, you can do this with friends or family or your pet hamster. Remember: 20 minutes.

❑ Write in a **group.** Invite other aspiring writers to meet and write together. Use some of the writing exercises (above) and complete two activities at once!

14 Because I love the night sky

One of the few places where science and romance come together – Astronomy. Who can forget the scene in *A Beautiful Mind* where Russell Crowe (as John Nash) traces the constellations in the night sky for Jennifer Connelly? Who knows? These activities might help you impress a date – not to mention your kids and your grandchildren. It's a good review, whether you're planning a cruise or camping trip (and a great excuse to spend some time gazing up into the sky.) The best way to start, according to the experts? Look up!

Complete the first two activities, plus four others.

❏ Read an **Astronomy magazine** for *three* months. Good ones include *Sky & Telescope* (www.skyandtelescope.com) and *Astronomy* (www.astronomy.com). These are available at your local newsstand or library.

❏ Be able to **identify** the following in the night sky:

North Star – why is this star important to navigation?

At least one planet

Six constellations

❏ Learn the **lingo**. Be able to explain the following basic Astronomy terms and how they're used when looking at the night sky. You can find their definitions and examples for usage on the magazine Web sites above, at the library or by asking a knowledgeable friend or acquaintance:

Sky measures	Angular measure	Arcminutes
Arcseconds	Sky coordinates	Celestial sphere
Declination	Right ascension	Celestial equator
Magnitude	Astronomical unit (a.u.).	Light-year parsec

❏ Visit a **planetarium** in your area. There are over 700 planetariums around the world listed on www.lochness.com (links page). Or contact your local science center or university to find the planetarium nearest you.

❑ Visit an **observatory**. Observatories are usually located where the sky is dark. To find one near you, consult your local tourist bureau, your library or university.

❑ Go **stargazing** with a group. For these "star parties" you'll need, at a minimum, three things: warm clothes; dark, clear skies; and a red flashlight. You can also bring along a binocular and star chart. Ask for advice from the group leader. Find a public party through your local Astronomy club, planetarium or observatory.

❑ Compare a current **sky chart** or map for your area with the night sky at least *three* times during the course (preferably each month). These can be found on the Web sites associated with the magazines you are reading or at your local planetarium. Some newspapers list daily star maps, as well. You can register on-line with www.astronomydaily.com for star charts personalized for the night sky in your location. You can also find an array of star charts and maps in the books about Astronomy listed in the following exercise.

❑ **Read** a book about Astronomy, such as:

- *Bright Star Atlas 2000* by Wil Tirion

- *Bad Astronomy: Misconceptions and misuses revealed, from Astrology to the moon landing "hoax"* by Philip C. Plait

- *A Field Guide to Stars and Planets* by Jay M. Pasachoff

- *Peterson First Guide to Astronomy* by Jay M. Pasachoff

- *The Star Book* by Robert Burnham

- *Secrets of the Night Sky: The most amazing things in the universe you can see with the naked eye* by Bob Berman

- *365 Starry Nights: An introduction to astronomy for every night of the year* by Chet Raymo

- *The Stars* by H. A. Rey

- *Exploration of the Universe* (textbook) by George Abell, David Morrison, and Sidney Wolff

- *Beginner's Guide to Amateur Astronomy* by David J. Eicher

Or, ask a friendly astronomer for a recommendation.

❑ Learn to use a **planisphere**. These are used in lieu of a star atlas. A planisphere is a two-layer disk-shaped tool that can show how the stars move through the sky. The top, rotating layer has an opening to reveal the constellations imprinted on the layer beneath. By turning the top layer and matching the month and hour scales along the circumference, you can get a sense of the motion of the constellations in the sky during the course of an evening. They are intended for naked eye observing.

❑ Participate in **National Dark Sky Week** (NDSW), held annually in April. This is one week each year when everyone in the United States helps reduce light pollution temporarily by turning off unnecessary lights. The idea is to step back for a moment and realize the wonder that our universe holds. It is supposed to encourage more-effective, less-obtrusive lighting systems. For the current year's date and more information, ask at your local observatory or go on-line to the National Dark Sky Week Web site at www.darksky.org.

❑ **Memorize** the planets' names and order. This mnemonic might help: Mother very thoughtfully made a jelly sandwich under no protest. (Earth is "t" for Terra and "a" is an asteroid belt!)

❑ Read the **mythology** behind at least two constellations and be able to tell their stories. The mythology can be Greek, Norse, Native American, Chinese, etc.

❑ These are tough activities to complete. Congratulate yourself by visiting a restaurant with at least one **Michelin star** (or in the US, at least 4 AAA Diamonds).

Elizabeth: *"I was in a rut with no inspiration to get out and do something: my job, my relationship and social life included. I wasn't depressed, but just stuck. When you are around a dynamic group of women it can't help but rub off. I was inspired by their experiences and accomplishments – it was kind of a kick in the pants. While trying to accomplish my goals, I started to accomplish other goals that I didn't even choose. It really was a big NO EXCUSE for sitting around. It's good to be around such an interesting and talented group of women."*

15 Because I want to try some new sports

These activities are designed to put a little variety into your workout – whether that variety is hiking instead of running, or walking around the block instead of around the mall. Or maybe you just need an excuse to pump up your performance in your favorite sport?

Complete three activities from below.

❑ **Train** for an event – whether it's a sponsored 3k walk with your dog or a marathon or a triathlon or a bike ride for a cause.

❑ If you're already working out, **substitute** one weekly session for something different. Do this four times during this course. This is not an additional workout, but a substitution. The changed workout does not have to be a completely new activity, but it does have to be different from "the usual." For instance, try trail running instead of city running; a different kind of yoga, etc.

❑ Try something **completely new**: soccer, Bikram yoga, biking, in-line skating outside, roller-skating inside, kite surfing, aqua-aerobics, ice skating, horseback riding, trail running, skiing, walking your dog (or a friend's), rowing, kayaking, punk rock or disco aerobics, tree climbing or even circus arts.

❑ Already an avid athlete? Try a sports camp or **group session,** especially if you participate in a lonely sport like running. This could be a six-week ski prep class in the fall or just a weekend run with a crazy running group like the international Hash House Harriers (www.gthhh.com). This is an excuse to mix it up with people who share your interest – and re-energize your workout with expert advice.

❑ Sign up for (and complete) a session with a **personal trainer**, no matter what your fitness level.

❑ Think of *five* sports, other than your "usual workout" that you've wanted to try or enjoy. Write each on a slip of paper. Fold these up and put them in an "exercise jar." Empty the jar by drawing a different **cross-training** sport *five* times during the course.

❏ Set a measurable **goal** to improve your mileage, your time, how much weight you can lift or your workout length. Make this an ambitious goal – one that could take the entire three-month course to reach. Give yourself incremental goals along the way. Attain the goal.

❏ If you normally run or walk inside on a treadmill or Stairmaster, take your workout to the streets (or trails) **outside** at least *four* times during the course to complete this activity.

❏ Participate in a **charity** sporting event.

16 Because I feel the need to create

Are you an enthusiastic starter of any kind of project? Do you have the closet full of fabric, patterns, dried flowers, beads, sequins, gourds, egg cartons and yarn to prove it? This is your excuse to take inventory and, hopefully, make progress on those projects. It's also a great excuse to complete a project in a new hobby area!

Complete the first activity, plus at least three more:

❏ Life is a work in progress, but sometimes you do need to finish something. What craft supplies do you have in your workroom/ bedroom/guestroom/garage/cellar/attic? This is your excuse to take **inventory.** Consolidate, count and quantify what you have. If you dare, make a monetary valuation of your loot. Now you know where you stand before you start any new projects. *Remember: Accumulation is not the same as creation!* (Although it sometimes feels just as good.)

❏ Free one project from the inventory above by **completing it.** Finish the baby quilt before the baby's all grown up. Weave a couple of placemats instead of a table runner. Put the photos in the scrapbook (see *Excuse #11: Because I want to walk down memory lane*). Just rekindle the excitement for one of the projects and finish it!

❏ Attend a **craft class.** As in Excuse #11, only purchase what you will use immediately – yarn for one sweater, beads for one neck- lace, etc. Better yet, attend a class where you leave with your finished project.

❏ Do you remember Popsicle stick log cabins, finger painting and woven potholders? Revive one craft from your **youth** – something you enjoyed – and do it again. (You can do this in conjunction with the next exercise to kill two craft activities with one crafty stone...)

❏ Do a craft **with a child.** Introduce a child to a new craft, or work on a favorite craft activity. The purpose of this exercise is to recap- ture a childlike enthusiasm for creation. (And you'll probably get to make a mess, as well.)

❏ Craft in **a crowd:** Go to a stamping party (but remember your mantra: "Accumulation is not creation."); test out a Stitch 'n' Bitch group (is your gossip good enough?); or get some people together to make tree ornaments. The excuse is to get together with like-minded people and create something!

❏ Do one project that costs you **no money.** This usually means using supplies that can be found around the house or in nature. Complete this project. (This is separate from using supplies you purchased previously, in the second exercise.)

❏ **Organize** your craft items. This is your excuse to doll up your doll-making space (or *whatever* else-making you're up to). Make it a pleasant space, but well thought-out, too.

❏ Make a **gift** for someone.

❏ **Practice** your craft for *one hour each week* during this program.

❏ Practice your craft for one hour **without any distractions** – TV and radio off; no background music. Where does your mind wander? Are you more focused on your work or more creative or less stressed? Do this *three* times during the program. (You can combine this with the exercise above.)

❏ **Teach** a craft to someone new. Maybe you can lead a group at the senior center or show your friends how to make those beaded bracelets they're always admiring on you. The goal is to pass on your passion and skills to someone new.

❏ Create a **holiday-themed craft.** This activity only counts if you finish the craft *before* the holiday.

❏ Make a craft for a **charitable organization.** This could mean putting together items to be used in a shelter or selling your crafts at a charity bazaar or even participating in a knit-a-thon. Whatever you do to complete this activity, have it make a difference in someone's life. (Get a group together and you can complete two activities at once!)

❏ Ask someone to **teach you a craft.** Let your friend or relative share his or her skills with you. Have a good visit while you're working together.

❑ **Sell** a craft item. You've always meant to and people are always saying you should. Figure out your cost, your price and find a buyer. How does it make you feel (other than wanting to rush out and buy more supplies)?

❑ Join an **organization** based on your favorite craft. How about the Gourd Artist's Guild or a Stitch 'n' Bitch group? Find one based on your skill level (or aspire to be better) and share the experience.

❑ Buy a **craft kit** and complete it.

❑ **Display** or wear one of your craft items. This doesn't mean put your woven potholders on your head, but it wouldn't hurt to flaunt that sweater vest you just finished crocheting.

Excuses to Please
(if only yourself)

Not that the other excuses won't please you, but these will give you pleasure just by being able to utter the words, "I'm sorry, I can't, because I am required to have a manicure/pedi-cure/massage/bubble bath/magnum of Moet tonight. I'll get back to you."

17 Because I need to survive in the city

You know the situation. Someone exclaims in an over-excited and over-interested voice:

"Oh, you're from Seattle/Minneapolis/Omaha/Tampa/ Amsterdam? I've always wanted to visit! What's there to do in Seattle/Minneapolis/Omaha/Tampa/Amsterdam?"

And you hem and haw and finally stammer:

"Well, all I ever see is my home, my office and the inside of the mall … I'm afraid I'm not much help."

Yes, your answer is pitiful – but not exactly rare. These activities are designed to purge that answer from your repertoire; to make you an expert on your own town; to make your knowledge as valuable as the well-tipped concierge at your city's top hotel.

Complete at least five tasks (so that, next time, you're prepared with the answers):

❑ *Where should I **stay?*** True, you rarely stay in a hotel in your own town (unless, of course, the plumbing's out or your house is being fumigated). Now's the time for a little research. Ask your friends and co-workers for recommendations. Where do business associates stay who come into town? Check out the travel section of your local paper for reviews or a local hotel guide (don't forget on-line resources.) Then VISIT a few of the hotels. Have a coffee in the lobby and observe the clientele. Ask to see a room "for a friend who's planning to visit." Then, complete these sentences with current information:

- The top-of-the-line, most elegant, biggest splurge hotel in my town is…

- A reasonably priced, clean, well-located hotel I'd recommend is…

- There's a little hotel (or bed & breakfast) that few people know about called…

❑ *Where should I **eat?*** Do you dream of reviewing restaurants for a living? Here's your chance to live the fantasy. Do the research via the newspaper, Internet and friends, but remember, you actually have to visit the restaurant to give an honest recommendation. Whether you just stop by for dessert or a drink in the bar or go for a whole meal is up to you. (This is a tough, grueling assignment!) Be able to recommend at least *three* from the following list:

- A romantic restaurant

- A family restaurant

- A vegetarian restaurant

- A restaurant with a killer view

- A restaurant with a hot chef (know his/her name)

- The top-rated restaurant in town or the restaurant everybody's talking about

- A neighborhood favorite

- A secret restaurant (one that hasn't been written up in the press)

- A place to taste local cuisine

- An all-night or after-hours restaurant

- A great place for breakfast

- Some place that serves a quick lunch

- A restaurant that you think is special because...

❑ *What should I **do*** in your town? Check out tour books for your city/state, the local *What's On* section of the newspaper and your friends' experiences for ideas. Remember, before you recommend an activity, you must do it yourself. Be able to recommend at least *four* from the following list:

- A good activity with kids

- A romantic activity

- A walking tour

- A bus tour

- A free activity

- A local art museum

- A local history museum

- A local science museum

- A visit to a landmark (St. Louis' Arch, Seattle's Space Needle)

- A museum catering to a local industry

- Your own category

❑ *If I do* **one thing**, *what should it be?* What is your favorite activity in your city? It may be taking in a view, a museum, a nightclub, or a store. Now, do that activity one more time (for the sake of research!).

❑ *Where should I* **shop?** Name *three* stores or shopping areas unique to your town. (You may NOT include any chain stores unless they are flagship stores.) Think antique stores, flea markets, boutiques, and farmers' markets. Here's your excuse to think outside the mall.

❑ *How do I* **get around?** Pretend you're from out of town – without your car. How will you get around? Hail a taxi. Get on the bus. Ride the metro or a new streetcar. Rent a bike – better yet, hire a Segway or pedi-cab. For this activity, try one new (or seldom-used) mode of transport.

❑ *So, what should I do* **at night?** Watching *Everybody Loves Raymond* reruns is not a valid answer here. Check out your *What's On* section again or go on-line. Try out and recommend at least *three* from the following list:

- A jazz club

- A dance club

- A cinema (anything unique in your town?)

- An evening tour (pub crawl, mystery tour, night sights)

- A great place to watch a sunset and have a drink

- A quiet bar

- A noisy bar

- An all-night or after-hours restaurant

- Your own category

❑ *When is the **best time** to visit?* Of course, you can already describe the weather, but do you know when the local festivals are? Put together an annual schedule of major festivals in your town (you can often find these in tour guides or on-line). Then, pencil *three* of them onto your calendar for the coming year – and attend them! Be sure to choose at least one that you have never attended.

❑ ***What's new** since the last time I visited?* Look back at your town's last couple of years. Have any new neighborhoods or areas been developed? Have any museums or attractions opened? Is there a new stadium or art exhibit or something else everybody's been talking about? If so, visit it and see if it lives up to the hype!

❑ *What's a good **guidebook?*** Buy or borrow at least one guidebook about your town or state and read it.

18 Because I'm really a Bad Twin inside

Here's your excuse to be the bad twin for once. Take a look at these activities. If you do not have to make any life changes in order to complete the tasks, then these activities are probably *not* for you – you probably are the bad twin. If you couldn't even imagine doing most of the activities – if you are most definitely the good twin – then they are *unquestionably* meant for you. The actions here are designed to give those of us who are just a little too tightly wound several excuses to unwind a bit (or *a lot*!). (And the author is not responsible for the consequences!)

**Complete the first activity, plus four more:
(For the overachievers out there, why not complete all the activities?)**

- ❑ For this exercise you will need **21 index cards** – 21 excuses to get out of doing something you don't want to do. On each card write "BAD TWIN." Every morning take one of the cards with you as you start the day. When you face something you do not want to do (a meeting, an errand, a trip to the dentist, a phone call, a work-out) take the card and use it. Is that your next-door neighbor on the phone again, whining about her husband? Wave the card in the air and say, "I'm sorry, I just can't talk right now. Goodbye!" Is your gym bag staring at you from the corner? Tuck your card into a side pocket and go out for a beer. Feel like skipping that meeting? Prop the card up next to your computer screen and surf the Web for an hour instead. Do not use more than one card per day. Use them all. (You have three weeks' worth of cards.)

- ❑ **Do not make your bed** for a week. Do not pull the comforter up to cover the mess – just leave it when you get out of bed in the morning. Think of it as an efficiency exercise. If your partner insists on making it, don't fight it. The key is for *you* to let it be.

- ❑ Get something **pierced or tattooed.**

Susan: *"I'm an overachiever. I'm going to try to not to make my bed for two weeks, not just one."*
(week one)

"I told my co-workers that I had appointments outside the office for the afternoon and spent three hours in Ikea! My boss called when I was there and I told him I was walking between appointments."
(week eight)

❑ Celebrate **junk food** day. This is one activity where your family will want to join you. Choose one day and give yourself permission to eat whatever you want. Full-fat. High-cholesterol. Sugar-coated. No decaf. No organic anything. Just eat crap for 24 hours. And remember – bad twins feel no guilt. (Although they often feel queasy.)

❑ Use them, don't lose them. Did you carry over **vacation days** from last year? Bad twins don't do this. Here's your excuse to take time off *now*. If you carried over too many days to use up during the 12-week course, schedule them into the next few months (*officially*) using whatever method you have to use at work. Fill out the form. Send the memo. Then – USE THEM!

❑ Wear your **naughtiest underwear** – the stuff you save for seduction – underneath your work clothes, your workout clothes, your uniform. If you don't own any wicked underwear, either go out and buy some – or don't wear any at all.

❑ Go to an **X-rated** movie, or watch one on DVD or cable.

❑ **Quick and bad.** Complete *three* of the following for this activity.

- Sleep naked.

- Go to bed without cleaning the kitchen. Leave the dirty dishes for the morning. Do not strategically soak them overnight.

- Don't take your vitamins for a day.

- Order a drink with a nasty name. Have some fun and do this when you're out with your in-laws. Or, better yet, order a round of them when you're out with the boss.

- Seduce your partner in the morning, even if you're both late for work.

- Is somebody at your door that you don't want to see? Hide.

- Go through the express lane at the grocery store with three extra items – on purpose.

- Throw away something that could be recycled.

- Mess up your cutlery drawer – put the spoons with the knives and leave them there for a week.

- Drink real coffee at night without worrying about the consequences. If you're awake at 3 am, find something naughty to do.

- Screen your calls for 24 hours. Don't talk to anybody you don't want to.

❏ Take a **two-hour lunch**. If you have to time yourself, that's okay. If the lunch goes over two hours, that is okay, as well.

❏ You're excused! Take a *"mental health"* day (Call in sick and go out and play). You don't have to advertise this to co-workers or family – just do it. If you don't work outside the home, arrange to have someone cover your car-pool, your errands, etc. and take the day off. (Maybe you have a neighbor with whom you could trade "days off.")

❏ Take a **meeting** – with yourself. Schedule a "meeting outside the office" and go window-shopping. Skip the PTA meeting and see a film.

19 Because I'm game for dating

You can complete these activities even if you're married! They are designed to get you out of the "let's do lunch" mode – where you say you'll get together with someone, but you never do. It's your excuse to take action: To get off your butt and do the things you're always saying you want to do. To make you dial the telephone and schedule some time with your friends. *To make the date!*

There are only four activities. They're really simple. You must do all four:

❏ Make a list of **10 activities** you want to do in the next three months. Here are some examples:

- See (name a movie):

- See (name a play):

- Eat dinner at (name a restaurant):

- Go out for breakfast at (name a café):

- Do lunch at (name a restaurant):

- Attend (name a musical event):

- Attend (name a festival):

- Listen to (name) speak:

- Go see the (sports team) play:

- Shop at (name a mall, a specific shop, etc):

- Visit that new (shop/restaurant/museum/race track) that opened:

- See the (name an exhibit) at the (name a museum):

- Go to the (name a place) one more time before they tear it down:

- Walk/jog/bike that (name a trail) I've always meant to try out:

- Visit that (name a spa) I've heard so much about:

- Ride that new (ferry/streetcar/roller coaster):

- ?

❑ Make a list of **10 people** with whom you've been meaning to get together. These can be new acquaintances, old friends or co-workers, family members – anyone who you "keep meaning to call."

❑ This is most difficult step. Get out your calendar and your telephone directory and **make a date** with at least *three* people from the "people" list to do three separate activities from the "activity" list. You can come clean and tell them about your "excuse," or just let them be happy to hear from you. You can match an activity to a person beforehand or let them choose from the list. Remember, you're probably more motivated about this than the people you're calling. If they balk at the invitation, say "thanks anyway" and move on down the list (in a diplomatic fashion) until you've made three dates. Schedule the dates throughout the three-month period.

❑ Now this is the fun part – **keep all three dates.**

20 Because I like my wildlife indoors

The key to exploring under the covers is that not all the exploration takes place under the covers. These activities are designed to add some fun to your sex life.

Complete at least four activities below:

❑ If you have a **television set** in your bedroom, here's your excuse to get rid of it. Move it out for an entire week. If it's too complicated to move, cover it with a pretty tablecloth and lock the remote in the trunk of the car. Replace David Letterman with someone just as fun.

❑ Take your partner to watch the **"submarine races"** or whatever you used to call them or even to a drive-in movie (preferably one you've already seen). Remember what it's like to maneuver around a stick shift. Climb into the back seat if you want. Does it re-ignite some pubescent passion, or just make you appreciate the king-size bed at home?

❑ Watch an **X-rated film**. If you're not ready to go for a XXX, there are all kinds of films, as well as guides to figure out exactly what level of "steam" you're seeking. Web site www.libida.com rates their selections by: "educational," "plot + sex," "R-rated," or "wall-to-wall sex," for example. You choose the film – especially if you're watching it with a friend.

❑ Read an **erotic novel**. *O* magazine recommends these series, especially for women: *Herotica* (Plume; Down There Press), *Best Women's Erotica* (Cleis) and *Sweet Life* (Cleis). What were the steamiest scenes? Why? Read them aloud to your partner for extra credit. Act them out for even more!

Myia: *"I worked on Excuse #20 on my vacation to Venice. It just made the week so much more fun and romantic. My husband thanks you."*

❤

❏ Organize a **week of passion** with your partner. Using a weekly planner split the week, with each of you taking responsibility for three or four days. Now, what do you do with your days? Laura Corn (www.foreplayforcouples.com) gave these suggestions in *Redbook* magazine: Write sexy little notes on "your" days; have a night of passionate sex without penetration; surprise your partner in the morning shower – jump in wearing a T-shirt and nothing else; get the kids out of the house and spend some time naked together around the house; keep the lights (or your panties) on during sex; or make up your own activities. (*Redbook* is way more than just Jell-O recipes these days!)

❏ List the 10 **sexiest people** you can think of – you don't have to know them personally; they can be celebrities, models, or passersby. Or they can be people you know: your husband, your boss, your mechanic. Male or female. Write down exactly what is sexy about each of them. What does this tell you about your own views of sex appeal?

❑ Neck with your **clothes on,** preferably at a movie or in your recreation room, but wearing pajamas in bed counts, too. Extra points for getting away with this while the kids are awake.

❑ **Tell your partner** what excites you. Be direct; mind reading doesn't always work! Take a deep breath and say, "This is what I want, or at least think I want." Then do it. Remember, you have the perfect excuse to bring the subject up!

❑ Buy – and use – a **sex toy.** If you already have a drawer full, try something new. Nowadays, you can do this via the Internet (Toys in Babeland (www.babeland.com) delivers their products in brown wrappers) or even through home parties! Others who claim to have thousands of representatives selling their products in living rooms across North America:
Pure Romance (www.pureromance.com),
Passion Parties (www.passionparties.com),
Slumber Parties (www.slumberparties.com)
and Fantasia (www.fantasiaparty.com)

Or, as author Anne Lamott recommends, visit your local drug store and purchase a massager made for sore necks (the packages all have smiling women on them). If you're into status, Myla (www.mylalingerie.com) is the first luxury sex-toy purveyor (across from Cartier's in NYC) or you can always stop by your neighborhood sex shop to ask for in-person advice.

❑ Read a *"how-to"* book. Nobody's born an expert; research counts. How about *The New Kama Sutra,* by Richard Enerson?

❑ Take a **bath with your partner.** Set the mood with candles and music. Lock the bathroom door. If your home bathtub isn't big enough for two, enquire when you book your next hotel room about the size of their tubs and complete this activity on the road.

❑ Add **five sensual things** to your life. This could include home furnishings (velvet, fur, leather, a dimmer switch, candles); food (chocolate that's not affiliated with a cartoon character or anything a child would not eat – fois gras, champagne, caviar); music (something that stirs your soul – turn off CNN and turn on some Bolero as a background to your housework!); art (whatever floats your boat), etc.

❑ Research and test a traditional **aphrodisiac.** (If your definition of "traditional aphrodisiac" includes anything advertised during the evening news or via the Internet, please get your doctor's approval!)

21 Because I need a little peace and spirituality

Spirituality means different things to different people. Here's an excuse to explore several areas, as well as put some peace into your life.

Complete at least four of these activities:

❑ If you do not regularly attend church, synagogue or mosque, visit your own **place of worship** at least *three* times during this program.

❑ Visit a different church, synagogue or mosque. Preferably this will be **outside your own faith**. Ask a friend if you can attend with him or her. What are the differences to your usual place of worship? If you do attend with a friend, be sure to extend the same invitation to visit your place of worship.

❑ Visit a psychic or medium and have a **reading**. If there is a free demonstration in your town, go along and take part.

❑ **Meditate.** Research shows that regular meditation can lower blood pressure, decrease anxiety, improve immune functions, increase vitality and improve sleep. Try at least two of these options to get started.

- *Mindfulness meditation:* This type of meditation focuses on breathing. Sit in a comfortable, upright position. If you're in a chair, place your hands in your lap and your feet flat on the floor. If you're on the floor, sit cross-legged. Close your eyes and take three or four deep, slow breaths. Then breathe gently until you feel a sense of peace and calmness. When thoughts arise (as they invariably will) notice them, then let them go. Start with five minutes (about the time it takes to quiet your thoughts) and build to at least 15 minutes daily. Do this *three* times. The website www.contemplativemind.org provides more specific instructions for this and the ambient noise meditation below.

- *Ambient noise meditation:* This type of meditation encourages you to embrace the sounds around you, instead of blocking them out. Great for a noisy house or office. Sit comfortably on a cushion on the floor or in a chair. If you commute by train or bus, you can do this en route to and from the office. Close your eyes, relax your shoulders, breathe gently and pay attention to the sounds around you: birds chirping, electricity humming, traffic outside the bus. Listen to them so deeply that your body can "hear" the vibration deep inside, feeling the sounds viscerally, not emotionally. If thoughts come up, let them go and re-focus on the sounds. Sit like this for at least 15 minutes. Do this meditation *three* times.

- On-line meditation: Believe it or not, you can access meditation tapes via your computer. The Web site www.learningmeditation.com has short meditations for everything from a short work break, a restoration exercise, a mini-getaway and a discovery for your inner guide. Do at least one exercise per day for *three* days.

- Use a meditation CD, video or DVD *three* times a week for *two* weeks. Often these can be checked out at a library or borrowed from friends.

- If you already meditate regularly, continue with your usual practice. Be sure to meditate *three* times each week during this course.

❑ This activity involves **praying** every day. It doesn't matter to whom you pray, how long it takes, or what you say. The important part is to acknowledge a spiritual being. You may want to recite prayers from your youth or from a different faith than you are used to. You may want to ask for guidance, strength or just say a prayer of thanks. You have a total of over 70 prayers (7 per week x 12 weeks) to send during this course; you should be able to fit them all in.

❑ Visit a **place that is sacred** to you. This could be a spot in nature that inspires. It could be the inside of a cathedral. It could be a favorite tree outside of town or a museum. This activity is two-fold. The first half is taking the time to make the journey – the pilgrimage – to this place. The second half is taking the time to enjoy it. Sit quietly for 30 minutes and do just that.

❑ Make a **personal sanctuary.** Find a spot in your home or garden and transform it into an oasis for yourself. It can be a whole room or just a corner – some place where the light appeals to you. Remove all unnecessary objects. Add candles or potpourri or music. Use it as a reading nook, a meditation spot, or just a place to retreat and regain your calm.

❑ If there is a **religious holiday** during your course time, observe it by relishing in its spiritual meaning. Don't pass over Passover. Don't miss midnight mass to wrap presents. Don't bend the tenets of Ramadan to suit your schedule. Whatever your faith, celebrate it.

❑ Get to know your neighbors. Investigate the **demographics** of your town, neighborhood or city. What are the major religions? Who worships where? Where are the churches, synagogues and mosques? You might be surprised at what you find.

❑ Try a **yoga** class. If you already do yoga, try a new type of yoga. Do this *four* times during the course.

❑ Do something tangible to **physically release** you from your day: Get a massage or go floating in an isolation tank.

❑ Walk a **labyrinth.** A labyrinth is a single path or tool for personal, psychological and spiritual transformation. Labyrinths are thought to enhance right brain activity. You make your way through the maze-like path as you think, meditate or pray.

❑ Grab a **pleasure morsel.** Do one of the following (or similar) non-essential pleasures *10* times during the program:

- Feed the ducks.

- Color with crayons.

- Take a break and read a chapter of a good book (this is not your "normal reading time," but a sneak read during your day, etc.).

- Blow soap bubbles.

- Sing out loud.

- Tell a joke.

- Walk in the rain (by choice).

- Swing on a swing or play on another piece of playground equipment.

- Ride your bike with "no hands."

- Ride a roller coaster or Ferris wheel.

- Practice *dolce far niente*, doing nothing, for five minutes.

- Play with a pet.

- Climb a tree.

- ???

❑ **Do not watch** television for at least one week. (Seven days. 168 hours.) If your family is watching, ask them to help you with this activity by turning off the television or go to a different area of the house.

22 Because I deserve to be pampered

Finally, you have an excuse. *"Sorry, I can't be there/do that. I "must" have a massage/facial/pedicure..."* Feel like a queen? Good, that's the point of these (extremely popular) activities.

Complete five of the following activities: (but feel free to do them all!)

❑ Have a **massage**. It can be a Swedish, Hot Stone, Shiatsu, Reflexology, Reiki, Watsu or Sports massage. Already a massage connoisseur? Then try something new!

❑ Soothe yourself with a **facial**. Close your eyes and relax and emerge with a glow.

❑ **Take a walk.** Don't walk the dog. Don't walk to the Post Office. Don't powerwalk. Just walk for at least 30 minutes with no purpose other than to go for a walk. Walk around your neighborhood (especially if you haven't for awhile). Stop at a pretty park on your way from (or to) the office. Walk while your daughter's at her ballet lesson. Just take some time to yourself and enjoy the scenery. Do this *four* times during the course to complete this activity. (Oh, and don't forget to turn off your cell phone!)

❑ Have a **pedicure.** Take a load off your feet. Be sure to choose a pretty color for your toenails – and show them off afterwards!

❑ **Drink champagne** for no other reason than to celebrate today. Toast yourself.

❑ Have a **manicure.** If you're really lucky, you'll find someone who massages your hands, as well.

❑ Throw out your **holey underpants.** Replace them. Buy at least one pair from a store that does not sell tires.

❑ Buy yourself **flowers.** Do not buy the flowers that happen to be discounted today. Do not by the bouquet the interior designer prescribed for the entryway table. Buy the flowers you like – whatever appeals to you. Then, keep them close by – in your bedroom, at your desk, in the kitchen. Do this *four* times throughout the 12-week course. (On a budget? Remember, one solitary flower can be just as special as a bunch!)

- ❑ **Iron your sheets.** (Better yet, have someone else iron them.)

- ❑ Treat yourself to a **pretty coffee cup** – especially if you use one with your company's logo at the office. Each time you take a sip, remember to treat yourself kindly. (And make sure you wash it after you use it.)

- ❑ Clear out your **bathroom cabinet.** Keep only those items you currently use. Organize them attractively. If you have bath oils, silky body creams or scented candles languishing in there – use them!

- ❑ **Take a bath** with bubbles, candles, music (and a glass of wine wouldn't hurt).

23 Because I need a weekend (or two)

These activities are for procrastinators – those of you who are sitting on your couch on a Sunday night and realize that you've just spent the weekend getting ready for the workweek ahead. These activities are designed to get you looking forward to the weekend's activities (and I'm not talking about ironing here!).

Complete all three activities:

❑ Read the ***What's On*** section of your newspaper. Usually newspapers run a special section featuring upcoming cultural events each week. Read this section every single week during the course. With a big marker (a red felt-tipped pen will do) CIRCLE each activity that interests you – no neat little highlights here. This section should speak to you now. Can you believe what you've been missing?

❑ After you've read the *What's On* section for two weeks, **list 10 things** you've always wanted to do in your town but you've never gotten around to doing. These can be things you've circled, or things that have been bumping around in your head for months or years. (Your newspaper circling exercise just serves as a stimulus.) Feel free to add to this original list of 10 as the weeks go by.

❑ Here's the hard part: **Do** at least *four* things from the list in the remaining 10 weeks of the program.

Lynn: *"Our cottage has always been a place of games, but over the past five years or so that has gone by the wayside. I resurrected that tradition this summer because of Excuse #38 (because I want to exercise my brain). I enjoyed it a lot and so did everyone that I dragged along."*

24 Because I want to sleep around (the world)

This is the kind of sleeping around that won't get you a reputation – except as a jet setter! With these activities you'll plan a trip to an exotic place – and what better excuse to visit?

Complete the first five activities below, plus two more:

❏ Choose a **country** you would like to visit.

❏ Plan an **itinerary** for a visit to the above country. Do not just purchase a guidebook, but actually find out the prices, opening times, etc. including:

- Hotel choices/prices – Read recommendations, check availability

- Transportation choices/prices – Airfare, ground transport, public transport, etc.

- Must-see sights

- Off-the-beaten track attractions

- Restaurants

- Museums – Any tips to avoid crowds? Discounts? Current exhibitions?

- Shopping

- Currency/exchange rates

- Visa requirements

- Tourist traps to avoid

❏ Identify *three* **famous people** from history who are associated with that country and *four* **famous events** that happened in that city. Read about them.

❏ Learn how to say "hello," "goodbye," "please" and "thank you" in the **local language**.

❏ Find at least one acquaintance who has visited the country and ask what his/her best and worst experiences were. Ask for **insider tips** and contacts.

❑ Use the itinerary above. **Book the trip** and go!

❑ **Read a book** about the country – fiction or non-fiction.

❑ Read a **travel guide** for the country that is at least 60 years old. (Do this in conjunction with Excuse #29.)

❑ Go to a restaurant that features the **cuisine** of the country or cook a meal using recipes from that country.

❑ Watch a **film** that was set in your chosen country.

25 Because I'm a Martha Stepford WannaBree

Throughout the ages, there have been many icons of proper woman-hood. No matter what was going on (or not) on the inside, on the outside these women seemed to be in control of everything from their cutlery to their cocktails. If your friends already call you "Bree" or "Martha" behind your back, this is probably not for you. But for the rest of us, these activities might bring a little civility back into our lives – at least on the outside.

Complete four activities below:

❏ Read a **book** about manners or etiquette. This can be anthropological (Claude Levi-Strauss' works); instructional (Emily Post); historical (anything from your mother's era); or even humorous!

❏ **Entertain** *three* times during the program, once each for brunch/breakfast, lunch and dinner. Send invitations or personally telephone each invitee. No email invitations! You can even host an "event" for just your family, but make sure they know it's special! The menu should be planned ahead of time for each meal, the table set properly, etc.

❏ Buy **thank-you notes.** Pick out a style that suits your personality. Now, for each invitation you accept during this course, send a thank-you note. (This might be a little over-the-top for some minor occasions, but it's always nice for the recipient to hear a "thank you.")

❏ Teach your children (or your partner – or yourself!) *three* rules of **etiquette** during the course – whether it's how to excuse themselves from the table properly, how to write a thank-you note, how to address elders when introduced, etc.

❏ Learn to **set a table** properly – placing cutlery, glasses, napkins, etc. correctly. Do this *10* times during the course for practice – even if it's just for yourself!

❏ Organize your **table linens.** Take each tablecloth or placemat out and ensure that they fit your current tables. Check for stains and tears. Throw any out (unless they are heirlooms) that are getting ratty. Donate or trade any that are the wrong size. Iron and/or launder each one and store where you can access them. Now use them!

- [ ] If your family doesn't normally **sit down together** for dinner, make it a point to do this *once a week* for the duration of the course.

- [ ] Buy a **negligee** and use it.

- [ ] Plan all your meals for a week and go grocery **shopping with a list**.

- [ ] Make a list of all friends and family members with birthdays and anniversaries during this course. **Send cards** ON-TIME for each event. Electronic cards do not count. Earn extra kudos for making the cards yourself.

- [ ] Rethink your housekeeping **supplies**: buy vacuum cleaner bag refills; introduce at least one new cleaning product into your home. Organize everything into an attractive carrier.

- [ ] Watch the original 1975 **Stepford Wives** movie *and* the 2004 remake for inspiration. Alternatively, you can read the book.

- [ ] **Bake** something from scratch. No mixes. Do this *four* times during the course.

- [ ] Meet your partner at the door with a **cocktail** after a long day. Do this *three* times during the course or until s/he says, "Enough!"

- [ ] Learn how to fold **dinner napkins** in *three* different ways. Use all three methods at least once during the course.

26 Because I need to stop and smell the roses

Sometimes it's hard to stop and smell the roses because there are no roses (or peonies or daffodils) around to smell! These activities are designed to bring some floral excitement into your life.

Complete four activities below:

❑ Learn the **names** of 10 kinds of flowers. These can be at the florist, in your garden, on a gardening show. Be able to identify them.

❑ Throughout the course, keep **fresh flowers** in your home or office. This means replacing them when they are dead – weekly, every other week, etc.

❑ Take a **flower arranging** course. If none is available, rent a DVD or ask a talented friend or family member for help (you bring the flowers; they bring the tips) – then try it yourself.

❑ **Replant** a small area where you spend a lot of time (or would like to) like a porch or a terrace. If it's spring, you get instant gratification; if it's fall, plant some bulbs and enjoy them later.

❑ Learn the following **gardening terms**: perennial, annual, pesticide, fertilizer, zone, compost, mulch, or any other term you've always wondered about.

❑ Plant an **herb garden.**

❑ Plant a **cutting garden.**

❑ Bring or **send flowers** to someone. Do this *three* times during the program.

❑ Visit a botanical garden or other **garden Mecca**. Notice the landscape design and the plant varieties. Take time to just smell the roses (or other flowers).

❑ Organize your **vases** and containers. Make sure they are clean and easy to access. If you have too many, fill them with flowers and bring them to friends (and tell them not to return the vase). If you never have quite the right vase, treat yourself to a new (or used via a flea market) one.

❑ Replace **dead houseplants**. Try something beautiful or exotic. Trim out-of-control vines. Fertilize and re-pot existing plants, if necessary.

27 Because I'm a closet gourmet

"Quality, not quantity." "Awareness." "Attention to detail." These are not the usual definitions of "gourmet," but they'll work here. These activities are designed to make you think about what you're putting into your mouth. Of course, they're also designed to let you eat a lot of good stuff, too!

Complete at least four activities below:

❏ Take a **cooking class.** You don't have to sign up for the *Cordon Bleu*, but this should be a course that emphasizes fresh ingredients as opposed to, say, the George Foreman Grill.

❏ Visit a **gourmet** or **kitchen** store. The key here is to not buy a thing. You are there on reconnaissance only. What ingredients or tools do they seem to specialize in? Ask the proprietor questions – you have the perfect excuse. If he/she could suggest one indispensable item for your kitchen, what would it be?

❏ Learn one **new recipe** from heart so that you can always create a healthy, fresh dish in a pinch.

❏ Outfit your **pantry** with the basics, depending on your cooking interests. Are you a baker? Do you cook Mediterranean or Asian? Do a little research and find out the five must-have staples for your kitchen and then stock them.

❏ They say cookbooks are to women what girly magazines are to men – you may never actually make the dish, but it's fun to imagine. Corrupt yourself with a little "**kitchen porn.**" Go to the cookbook section of your library or bookstore (or your own bookshelf, if you have your own stash) and browse new recipes. Try at least *three* new recipes you find in the cookbooks.

❏ For the duration of the course, buy only **local, fresh, in-season fruits** and vegetables. No more bananas in Minneapolis!

❏ Learn to recognize *four* different kinds of fish at the **fish market.** Try them all.

❏ Research the **restaurants** in your town. Visit at least *two* that are known for their excellent cuisine. Ask the waiter lots of questions and pay attention to the ingredients and preparation. Tip well.

❏ Sharpen all your **knives** and replace any dangerous ones. Learn one new chopping/slicing technique.

❑ Visit a local **culinary institute's** open day. Many schools open their cafeterias a few days a year so that their students can practice what they've learned. It's a great way to see where some of the best chefs started out – and usually at a reasonable price.

❑ Plan a **group cooking** day or evening. In some cities you can hire a chef to come in and direct an event in your home. Also, some cooking schools allow you to come into their schools and cook – and eat – for a night. If you have a chef in the family (or neighborhood), hire or cajole him/her into helping out. The key is to see where good food originates!

❑ Make **two salads**. In one salad, use only organic ingredients (including dressing). In the other use the usual supermarket offerings. Do you taste a difference? Does your family? Compare price and nutritional values.

❑ Prepare a multi-course meal, **matching wines** to each course. Alternatively, if you're more into the "eating" side of these activities, visit a restaurant specializing in wine pairing.

❑ Shop at a **farmer's market**. Do this *three* times during the course. Ask where the vegetables are grown, meet the producers and buy some fresh flowers. Notice what is in season.

❑ Go on a **chef's tour**. This can be a tour of a market, of specialty shops, of a kitchen, of an organic farm – anywhere you get a behind-the-scenes look at the world of food.

❑ Over the duration of the course, eat *six* **foods you've never tried** – from *foie gras* to fennel to horse. Did you find any new favorites?

❑ **Learn** how to do *three* of the following. You can find instructional videos at www.epicurious.com or use a cookbook or mother's/ friend's expert advice. You can substitute something else that you've been meaning to master in the kitchen, if you'd like:

- Check nuts for freshness
- Store fruit without browning
- Choose a good melon
- Blanche
- Fricassee
- Whip cream
- Make gravy or beurre blanc
- Poach an egg
- Sharpen a knife
- Clean mussels or de-vein a shrimp
- Identify fresh fish
- Boil water
- Make a roux
- Caramelize sugar
- Butterfly a leg of lamb
- Cut up a chicken or carve a turkey

28 Because I (ought to) love to shop

Here's your excuse to see what separates those women who live to shop and those women who would rather stick needles in their eyes than stick their body in a dressing room. Love to shop? You'll be right at home. Hate to shop? Maybe this will take some of the sting out of the experience (and start a new addiction).

Complete at least five activities:

❏ Read a **shopping magazine** (yes, they exist). Think of *Lucky, Shop Etc, Domino* (for your home) and their sister magazines as reconnaissance before the hunt. Do this *twice* during the program.

❏ Get to know **where to shop** in your town. Visit *three* major stores or shopping areas unique to your town. (You may NOT include any chain stores unless they are flagship stores.) Think antique stores, flea markets, boutiques and farmers' markets. What makes them unique? Do they live up to the hype? Do this in conjunction with *Excuse #17: Because I need to survive in the city.* This is your excuse to "think outside the mall."

❏ Find the best of the best. Make a **list of favorites.** They can be in your town or, if you are a real jet setter, all over the world! Here are some ideas, but you can make up your own categories. You should have at least *10*:

- I get the best, most personal service at _____.

- The most unique "junk" you'll ever find is the _____ flea market.

- Everything always fits at _____.

- Shoes? I always go to my favorite – _____.

- If you are looking for a specific piece (this could be jewelry, antiques, china), visit _____.

- I always take my mother/aunt/daughter to _____ when we're out for a special day.

- _____. They take back anything!

- Even my partner likes to shop at _____.

- They always have the latest style in stock: _____.

- They always have unique items that never appear in the magazines but always are just perfect! _____

- Lowest prices for _____? _____.

- _____ is expensive, but it's worth every penny!

- _____ delivers.

- _____ is the only place I've ever seen _____ and I couldn't live without them.

- _____ is my very favorite shop in the whole world.

❏ Go shopping on the **Internet**. If you're a first-time Internet shopper, buying one item on-line is enough to complete this activity. However, if you're already a savvy on-line shopper, you have to try harder: Try a shopping bot. A "bot" (short for robot) is a tool used to search through different Web sites. A shopping bot specifically searches all the on-line stores to identify who's selling the item you want and for what price. It then gives you data so you can compare prices. See www.froogle.com or www.alibris.com (for books). Or, complete an entire list of shopping (holiday, back-to-school, household outfitting) via the Internet.

❏ Try out a **personal shopper**. This can be an in-store service or an independent shopper. You can use the service for a gift for a client, your wardrobe, your boss's husband's birthday gift...

❏ Shop with strings attached. Make a purchase that is tied to a **charitable cause**. There are many ways to do this. You could shop at a store affiliated with an organization (Oxfam, Goodwill, the local hospital guild); you could buy something at a charity auction; or you could buy a product that sends a donation to a cause.

❏ Plan a **shopping trip** – really plan it. This is not a trip of errand running. This is SHOPPING! Research the area in your local paper or magazine. Make lunch reservations. Invite a friend. Plan your time for enjoyment – leave enough time for meandering through a flea market, trying on hats in a boutique – and don't forget that cup of tea/glass of wine at the end of the trip to relive your shopping adventure.

❏ Clip and use a **coupon**. If you're already a coupon-addict, take the time to organize your stash and then use a coupon.

❑ For the duration of the program, **greet the proprietor**/clerk when you enter a place of business. Don't be put off by their reaction (or non-reaction), just smile and say, "Hello. How are you today?" How did it change your shopping experience and your level of service?

❑ Have some commodity **delivered** to your home. This could be your heavy staples of grocery shopping ordered on-line, plants from a nursery or even an Ikea order. Treat yourself to the luxury of not hauling items home.

❑ Pretend you're a tourist in your hometown. Get a **guidebook** and read the shopping section. Visit at least *five* places that are recommended in the guide during the duration of the course.

❑ Take a **shopping vacation.** Visit a different town specifically for shopping. (Okay, you can take in a few sights while you're there.) This might be a pre-holiday blitz to the neighboring sales-tax-free state; a pilgrimage to an area known for a particular product (quilts, ceramics, glassware); a first-class flight to Istanbul for carpets; a day of outlet mall shopping or a visit to the Christmas Markets.

❑ Treat yourself to a **kid-free shopping** day (and treat your kids to a shopping-free day). Next time you are faced with dragging one child and pushing another through the mall, call the sitter/partner/aunt and leave the children at home. You could exchange days with a friend.

❑ Buy two **gifts out of season.** Make a specific trip to find the perfect gift for your father six months before his birthday. Make a dent in your Christmas shopping in July. Take your time and give yourself time to think about the gifts.

❑ Make a **shopping pilgrimage.** This could be to a flagship store of your favorite brand (Tabasco, REI, L.L. Bean, Hammacher Schlemmer) or some other notable destination (maybe the department store where you used to shop with your grandma?).

❑ Attend an **auction** in person. This can be at a big auction house like Christie's or Sotheby's or a local or specialty auction house. If you are serious about bidding, do your homework: attend the preview, read the catalogue, examine the merchandise, talk to a specialist, read any written condition reports, register to bid, figure your top bid (including any buyer's premiums, sales tax and delivery costs) and stick to it! Remember, printed estimates tend to be conservative!

29 Because I'm really a bookworm at heart

So you think you're a bookworm, do you? Or are you wondering what all the fuss is about? Why are all these people talking about books all of a sudden? Here's your excuse for guilt-free exploration into the pages of a good book, to a good book store or between the library stacks.

Complete the first activity, plus at least four additional activities:

❏ Obtain a **library card** – or renew your current one! In most cities and counties, this is free. All you have to do is provide proof that you live or work in the area.

❏ Now that you have your library card, learn how to **use the library**. Remember learning about the Dewey Decimal System in third grade? Things have changed. Most public libraries have user's tours that cover their (usually) free Internet access, community events, researchers at your beck and call, free access to expensive on-line databases and even free magazines! (Note – this exercise will help you IMMENSELY and save you money – throughout this program.)

❏ Read a **poem** every day for the remainder of this program. Great books to reference include: your college anthology that you never sold; any poetry assigned to your teenagers (it will make them crazy that you're interested); the *Poem a Day* series, published in both the US (Zoland Books) and UK (Random House); or switch between dead, live, local, translated, modern, traditional poets and poems each week. Just be sure to read *one poem every single day*! (Yes, it counts, if you can get your partner to read a sonnet TO you, as well.)

❏ List your *10* **favorite books**. How old were you when you read each one? Think about what you loved and remember the best parts. Reread one of the books (or at least your favorite passages). Recommend at least one of the books to a friend (better yet, give the book as a gift).

❑ You know the **book columns** in popular magazines that interview celebrities about what they are reading? Create your own. Do the same research about the celebrities in your own life. Start with yourself and pass questions such as these on to *five* people you care about:

- Which is your favorite book?

- Tell me a book you could not finish.

- Which fictional character would you most like to be?

- What's the most romantic book you've read?

- Has a book ever shocked you?

- Can you recommend a self-help book?

- What is your favorite book about motherhood/sisterhood/family/travel/love (choose your own topic)?

- Try to ask these questions in person, but if distance doesn't allow, email or telephone conversations count, as well. If you're in a book group – circulate the questions before your next meeting and lead the exercise as an opener.

❑ Make a **pilgrimage** to a book Mecca: get lost in Powell's City of Books in Portland, OR; be hep at City Lights Booksellers in San Francisco; photograph the lions in front of the NYC Public Library; take the architectural tour of Seattle's new Rem Koolhaas structure; have a coffee on the Left Bank in Paris … visit any place that means "books" to you.

❑ This activity is a little more narrowly focused than the previous one. View an original manuscript, an antiquarian manuscript or any **historically significant** piece of writing. This could be a local author's first draft in the public library archives; a *Star Trek* script at Indiana University's Lilly Library (they also hold the first published letter about the New World from 1493); the *Magna Carta* or the *Gutenberg Bible* at the British Library in London; any documents at a US presidential library, etc. Be original and see something interesting – maybe something that's been right around the corner for years!

❏ Buy a **special book**. This might be a first edition of a favorite or maybe it's a book from your childhood. Maybe it's a photo book of your favorite city – or a foreign book in its original language (whether you can read it or not). Make this a literary present to yourself.

❏ Try out a **book group** – or if you already attend one regularly, volunteer to *lead* an upcoming discussion. Read the book; prepare questions; do a little research into the culture or historical era of the book you read. Did you enjoy the book more by sharing it with other readers?

❏ Attend a major **book event,** such as a literary festival or convention like the Northwest Bookfest in Seattle, the American Booksellers Association Convention in Miami, the Frankfurt Book Fair in Germany, or any other local or regional convention.

❏ Get to know an **author.** If you've recently finished reading a book that made you curious about the author, this is your excuse to take the time and do the research. This could include reading his/her biography, reading essays or articles about or written by the author, watching a film about the author's life, listening to or reading interviews with the author, etc.

❏ Attend an **author lecture** and hear what the writer has to say about getting the book on the page. This should be more than just a book signing at a bookstore – this should be an opportunity to hear the author speak about the writing experience.

❏ **Write a letter** to an author whose book made a difference in your life and *send it.* You can find addresses on the Internet, either via the book's publisher or the author's agent, or his/her own Web site. Alternatively, if you are attending a book signing or lecture, give a short "thank you" in person and hand deliver a longer letter for the author to read later.

❏ Read the movie or **see the book.** If you've read a book and there is a film of the story, view it. If you've seen a film and there is a book version of the film, read it. You can also do both (read the book and see the film), time permitting, during this course.

❏   Read a book set in **your locale** (or a location you might be visiting soon). Make a list of places mentioned in the book and put together a tour. If you've just finished reading *The Diary of Anne Frank*, visit her neighborhood school in Amsterdam; or if you read Michael Connelly mysteries, make a tour of "his" Los Angeles. You get the picture!

❏   If you are traveling during this program, take along a **vintage travel guide** – and use it! Anything printed about European cities before WWI or WWII has a completely different focus than today's guides; travel advice for the Soviet Union is almost unrecognizable; and any European's adventures in the New World are especially entertaining. Just beware – the public transportation maps and hotel rates are generally useless! (Do this in conjunction with Excuse #24.)

❏   **Source** the same book at six different locations – a chain, an independent, a used-book store, a library, a warehouse store and on-line. Compare not only the price, but also the experience of buying the book. Was it easily available? Were you able to get advice about other books you might like? Could you get to take a look at the book before you took it home? Did you make human contact with other book lovers?

30 Because I AM a grown-up! I AM a grown-up!

So you no longer speak in full sentences, you carry a bag with teddy bears on it and your idea of a "quickie" is grabbing a nap while the kids sleep? Somewhere inside lurks a real adult. Here's your excuse to turn on something or someone other than *Barney* or the *Teletubbies*.

Complete at least five activities:

❑ List *10* **pre-kid activities** (however small) you used to enjoy with your partner – listening to LOUD rock 'n roll, playing cribbage or video games, showering together, slow dancing (even if it's in the living room), going out to dinner, having a nightcap, walking after dinner, having a real racy, romantic kiss ... This is your excuse to do at least *one of them each week* of the program.

❑ Reintroduce **adult music** into your life. When it's time to relax, swap a children's lullaby for one of *your* favorite soothing songs. As for car music, why not teach your kids the lyrics to *Cheeseburger in Paradise* instead of one more round of *Ten Little Monkeys*? You don't have to have the latest Eminem lyrics blasting, but it's not too early to introduce real music into your children's lives. Besides, they say classical music played at a young age can increase math abilities.

❑ Do you remember a time when you had an opinion on politics and knew what was going on in the world? This is your excuse to keep up with **the news.** For the remainder of the program, stay on top of the news (at least the headlines). If you cannot fit an entire read of the daily paper into your schedule, try one of these timesaving tactics.

- Scan the first three paragraphs of each story on the first page. News stories are written with the facts up front. This will give you a taste of the headlines. If you have more time, skip to your favorite section of the paper (from Op-Ed to *Cathy*) and read that, as well.

- Subscribe to an on-line summary of the day's news. If necessary, print it out and take it along with you to read while waiting in the doctor's office, while locked in the bathroom, or during children's hour at the library.

- Set your clock radio to wake up to the news and watch the first 15 minutes of the national newscast for the headlines each night.

❏ Have a **romantic dinner** at home. The food doesn't have to be elaborate, but set the table properly after the kids are asleep, light the candles, spray on some cologne and set the ground rules – no talk about the kids!

❏ Get your VEG-etables. If your errands have gotten the best of you, rent the kids a DVD, buy a couple of magazines, order in for dinner and just veg. This is your excuse to **do nothing** for an afternoon: no laundry, no errands, no cooking.

❏ Take a **"Marital Health Day."** Take a day off with your partner while the kids are at school. Feel a little illicit? That's the point!

❏ Read *at least one* **grown-up book** during this program – this does not include board books, *Goodnight Moon* or even *Counting Kisses: A Kiss & Read Book* (even if you're reading it naked to your partner).

❏ Send yourself away to **camp**, instead of the kids. If your children have a week or a weekend away, indulge yourself. A church-sponsored weekend retreat; an adult smart camp; a spa retreat; or just an overnight at your friends' lake cabin – they all count towards your camper experience.

❏ Schedule a **play date for yourself.** Instead of sticking around to watch the kids play on their play dates while making small talk, drop them off and do something for yourself. Trade the favor so the other mother can enjoy a play date, as well. Do this *twice* during the program.

❏ Make and keep a **weekly date** with your partner throughout the program.

❏ Take a **mini-break** during the day. Complete *two* of these mini-breaks from *Parenting* magazine *each week* during the program to complete this exercise. You can also think of your own breaks to include:

• Yoga break: Lie on your back with your legs up against a wall, so your body's in an L shape. Close your eyes and take slow, deep breaths. Try to maintain the pose for 5 to 15 minutes to ease muscle tension and replenish energy.

• Brain break: Do a crossword puzzle – a mini workout for your mind.

- Heartbeat break: Do something physical to raise your heart-beat – run up stairs, walk briskly to the mailbox, take a quick trip around the block, etc. (You may not count every trip up the stairs as a mini break!)

- Spa break: Soak a hand towel in water and wring it out, then warm the towel in the microwave for 60 seconds. To protect skin from direct heat, place a dry towel on your neck, then roll up the heated towel and lay it on top. Gently rotate your head back and to the sides as the heat works its way into your neck.

- Commuter break: Researchers at Stockholm University found that working women's stress and blood-pressure levels stay elevated after quitting time, so give yourself time to wind down before meeting up with your family. Take a detour past a park, stop at a bookstore, get off the bus one stop early and stroll home.

- Snuggle break: Take a few extra minutes in bed with your partner in the morning. Studies show this can raise levels of the stress-reducing hormone oxytocin, as well as lower blood pressure.

❑ Make a sacred **workout** schedule for the remainder of the course. Put the times on the calendar and make childcare arrangements ahead of time, if your gym doesn't have a day care. Keep to the schedule religiously – whether it's one day a week or seven – during the program.

❑ Meet for dinner, drinks or some kind of night out with other moms. The rule is: **No talking about children** – yours or anybody else's. Do this *twice* during the course.

❑ Make up **racy lyrics** to a favorite children's song. When the wheels on the bus have gone around one too many times, you can sing along (in your head) for a little private grown-up moment. Teach it to your partner for your own inside joke during play time with the kids. Don't forget to share it at the next get-together.

❑ Remember those **drinking games** in college? Here is one with a new twist. Every time you mention one of your kids – drink. You can work this into a dinner with other parents, mom's night out or even a night home with your partner. Be as strict as you'd like with the rules: Mention *your own* child and drink or *anybody's* child and you have to drink! Mention teething, diaper rash, sitter problems, lack of sleep and drink! Play this (at least) *once* during the course.

❑ **Schedule sex** (with your partner) and keep to the schedule – even if you're not in the mood. Remember, sex is like wine: even when it's bad, it's not so bad. Do this *three* times during the program.

Excuses to be Practical

These are the kinds of things that if you ever got around to doing would make your life better, but you need a friend to give you a kick in the rear (or a martini) to get going.

EXCUSE NUMBER

31 Because I need to get a handle on technology

Is technology taking over your life? Are you hanging precariously from a technology thread that threatens to snap every time you boot up your computer or try to dial your cell phone? These activities are designed to let you take control of the technology in your life.

Complete at least five of the activities below:

❑ If your VCR (or any electronic device) is **blinking** 12:00! 12:00! 12:00! this is the activity for you. Read the instruction manual and set the clock. In addition, set all clocks in your home and car to the same time. Remember how to do this for Daylight Savings Time changes. Mark the changeover dates on your calendar.

❑ **Back up** your computer. How many times have you told yourself you should? Or did you actually do it – *once*? There is plenty of good advice on how to do this. Many libraries have computer specialists on staff to point you in the right direction or you can find instructions in your manuals or on-line – try www.ehow.com. Now, depending on how much you use your computer, put this on your calendar every day, week, month, quarter, etc. and *stick to the schedule*!

❑ Your **cell phone.** You carry it everywhere; you should get to know it better. Here's your excuse to read the instruction manual without looking like a dweeb. Be able to:

- Use call waiting, forwarding and holding (if applicable).

- Access voicemail, including deleting messages. Update your greeting.

- Use the clock and calculator features.

- Change the ring and switch from ring to vibrate to flight mode.

- Access the Internet or email messages from your phone (if applicable and economical).

- Send a text or SMS message and receive one.

- Update your one-touch and/or speed-dial numbers.

- Are your phone numbers stored under names, or do you have to scroll through your call history to find a number? Update your phone directory.

Sheila: *"I'm the queen of the flashing 12:00! 12:00! 12:00! on every appliance. Last week I hit some button on my cell phone and now it only sends text messages in French. I have two DVD players at my place and I can't figure out which holes to use ... and the funny thing is, for the past 15 years I've worked in information technology! I need to do this excuse."*

- Do you want to allow people see your number when you call them? If not, turn on the privacy feature (if applicable).

- What would happen if you lost your cell phone, or it were stolen? Is there a password protection feature? If so, set it and remember it.

- Are you prone to *late-night, after partying* speed dialing to "re-connect" with old boyfriends, tell off ex-husbands or - bosses, or any kinds of calls you regularly regret in the morning? If so, devise an emergency *no-dial system*: enter a password that you won't remember after a few martinis (or only your roommate knows) or delete all possible late-night phone numbers before going out!

- Finally, do you know how much a phone call costs? What is your roaming area and charge? Analyze your calling plan to make sure it suits your lifestyle.

❏ Be safe when driving. Of the approximately 140 million cell phone subscribers in the US, only about 20 percent currently use hands-free devices. Using a handheld cell phone while driving is a crime in many countries and in several US states. Don't wait for it to become a law. To complete this activity, you must do *one* of the following:

- "Hang up and drive." Set your cell phone to voicemail when you're driving and quit making calls when you are on the road for the entire duration of this course.

- Buy a hands-free cell phone mechanism for your car and use it responsibly. There are many styles available, starting at around $15.

❏ Untangle the cords leading to all **electronic nests** in your house (around the PC, the stereo, the home theatre system, the kitchen). Organize them using cord tubes and wire ties (available at hardware and electronics stores). Replace any frayed cords and rethink any overloaded outlets. Install power strips with surge protectors, where necessary.

❏ Read and organize your **instruction manuals.** Create a file in your home of all of your seldom-used instruction manuals – kitchen appliances, stereo equipment, washer/dryer. Before filing them, choose *three* that you've never read and read them. You will be surprised at what you'll learn about not sorting cutlery in the dishwasher, etc. These are supposed to be laborsaving devices! Use all their features. For manuals you refer to frequently, store them near the appliances.

❏ Set the clock in **your car** and pre-set your radio stations. If you have a GPS or navigation system, learn how to use it. Change the batteries in your remote door lock control (or replace the unit, if necessary).

❑ Plan a **tech-free day** to show technology who's boss. Do not watch television, listen to the stereo or check your email. Shun all high-tech/convenience devices. Don't use the washing machine, dryer, dishwasher, microwave. Turn off your cell phone (you can leave a message that this is your "Amish Day.") No, you don't have to unplug the freezer, but a candle-lit evening is not out of the question. Do this *three* times during the course.

❑ Find **something human** to do with technology. Learn to send an SMS/text message to a loved one; put a racy photo of your partner on your screen saver; set up your partner's camera phone so that when it rings, you appear on the screen! To complete this activity, do one thing to put some humanity into your technology.

32 Because I need to tame my pocketbook

Believe it or not, some of you will consider this *fun*. Others will look at it as something you have *needed* to do for a long, long time. These activities are designed to introduce you to resources and make you take a look at your personal situation.

Complete the first activity, plus at least four of the others:

❏ Read a personal finance magazine for three months running. These are usually available at your library or newsstand. Some good ones include *Money* (www.money.com), *The Wall Street Journal's Smartmoney* (www.smartmoney.com) or *Kiplinger's Personal Finance* (www.kiplinger.com).

❏ Figure your **net worth.** This will be more fun for some than others, but either way, it's a great barometer for reading the current state of your finances. In a nutshell, you add up your assets (such as savings accounts, equity in your home, furniture, investments) and subtract your liabilities (credit card debt, outstanding mortgage or car loan amounts). There are specific worksheets available on the personal finance magazine Web sites above. Complete any of these (or similar worksheets) for this activity.

❏ If you have **investments,** find out about them – especially if you have a partner who regularly handles this area. Read prospectuses; visit Web sites; look at your statements; ask questions. Alternatively, if you are the spouse who regularly handles the family investments, you can also complete this activity by explaining them to your significant other.

❏ For one month, write down **everything you spend.** Visibility can be an affirming – or a humbling – state. If this sounds daunting, there is a shortcut. Pay for everything with a single card whenever possible – either a credit card (as long as you can trust yourself to pay it off at the end of the month) or debit card. Use cash for only very small purchases. Or, you can put the information in a computer program like *Microsoft Money* or *Quicken* (and kill two activities at once!). No matter which method you use, take time at the end of the month to analyze where your money is going. If you're unhappy with what you find, complete the last exercise listed.

❑ Balance your **checkbook.** If you're mature enough to have a check-book, you're mature enough to balance it!

❑ Make a list of your **credit cards,** the outstanding debt and the interest rate for each. According to financial experts, the key to getting out of debt efficiently is to pay off the highest interest cards first while paying the minimum amount on the other cards – but first, you need to know what you have. That darned visibility, again! If you're happy with the list – congratulations! If not, see the last activity listed.

❑ If you have a 401k or **savings plan** at work, investigate it and make sure you are maximizing its use.

❑ Switch to **on-line bill paying** or automatic deduction for on-going payments. Studies show that people who pay their bills immediately are happier than those who wait.

❑ Organize and **take control** of your finances with a computer program such as *Quicken* or *Microsoft Money*. By completing this activity you can conceivably kill two more "activity birds" with one stone: balancing your checkbook, as well as finding out your net worth.

❑ Analyze **your portfolio** in relation to your situation (age, retirement plans, dependents). The personal finance magazines you are read-ing, as well as their affiliated Web sites, are a goldmine of informa-tion in this area.

❑ Create a **money mission statement.** Susan Bradley, an American financial planner (www.womenmeaningandmoney.com), suggests this exercise to ensure that money does not rule your life, but feeds your own agenda. Your goal is come up with a touchstone state-ment (such as "Monterey" if your goal is to retire to a beach cottage in Monterey) by answering the following questions:

  • If you had very little time left to live, what would you most regret not having done, said, attempted or accomplished?

  • What has always been true of you, regardless of your age or stage of life – and what will probably always be true of you?

- Think of a time, whether it was in public or private, when you were most yourself, when you felt for a time or a moment that you were living the life you were meant to live.

- Mull these questions over for a few days or weeks. If you have a partner, answer them together. Come up with your statement by the end of the program and use it whenever you are making financial decisions, large or small.

❑ Set up a system for your **tax records** and keep to it all year (at least for the three months of this program!). You can find a good system in one of the magazines you're reading or on their affiliated Web sites.

❑ Need some **corrective measures**? What did you discover when completing the other activities? If you found that you need to make changes – do! You can consider making any of those changes as your fifth activity. For more information about seeking help, refer to the personal finance publications you've been reading. And remember, pat yourself on the back for taking a step in the right direction.

Noel: *"A group of women can go out, do 25 different things, but still come together and meet with a common purpose, all the while remaining authentic to what is of interest and importance in her own individual life. I think with the way people can hide behind email and the growing problems with social phobia, it is important to have books that bring people together socially."*

Noel learned to drive a stick shift for Excuse #37 (because I really, really need to do this).

33 Because I need to protect my identity

An identity thief obtains some piece of your personal information and uses it without your knowledge to commit fraud or theft – for example, opening a credit card account in your name. Identity theft is a serious crime. People whose identities have been stolen can spend years cleaning up their credit record. These activities will help you guard yourself against identity theft.

Complete the first activity plus three more:

❏ Order a copy of your **credit report** from each of the three major credit bureaus. Your credit report contains information on where you work and live, the credit accounts that have been opened in your name, how you pay your bills and whether you've been sued, arrested or filed for bankruptcy. Make sure it's accurate and includes only those activities you've authorized.

Equifax (www.equifax.com)
To order your report, call: 800-525-6285
or write P.O. Box 740241, Atlanta, GA 30374-0241

Experian (www.experian.com)
To order your report, call: 888-EXPERIAN (397-3742)
or write P.O. Box 9532, Allen TX 75013

TransUnion (www.transunion.com)
To order your report, call: 800-680-7289
or write: P.O. Box 6790, Fullerton, CA 92834-6790

❏ By US law, everyone in the US is entitled to one free credit report a year from each of the national credit agencies. More information about this law can be found at www.annualcreditreport.com or www.ftc.gov. Or, you can call 877-322-8228 or download an order form at the Federal Trade Commission site above. Note: The free credit reports need to be ordered via the FTC, not through the individual agencies.

❏ Place **passwords** on your credit card, bank and phone accounts. Avoid using easily available information like your mother's maiden name, your birth date, the last four digits of your Social Security Number or your phone number, or a series of consecutive numbers.

❏ Secure **personal information** in your home, especially if you have roommates, employ outside help or are having service work done in your home. Guard your Social Security Number jealously. Keep your card locked up and do not give out the number without a fight. (Usually when your number is requested, you can give alternate information instead, such as a driver's license number. Always ask.)

❏ Ask about information security procedures in your **workplace.** Find out who has access to your personal information and verify that records are kept in a secure location. Ask about the disposal procedures for those records as well.

❏ Reduce dangerous **paperwork.** Complete this activity by doing one or more of the following:

- Buy a crosscut shredder for documents and use it. (It's an excuse to throw a party with the confetti!)

- Request bills on-line, instead of via post.

- Get off mailing lists for pre-approved credit cards. In the US, call 888-5-OPTOUT.

- Ask financial firms not to trade your personal data. Privacy policies explaining how to opt-out are mailed each year. Ask that your data not be shared with affiliates or with outside firms.

❏ If your state allows a **freeze** on your credit ratings, sign up for that service. Many states now allow you to require that credit bureaus (see above) contact you whenever there is a request for your credit report. This makes opening a new credit report in your name more difficult – but it's worth it to deter identity thieves.

❏ This activity is designed to make you aware of your own actions. You don't have to don a trench coat and Audrey Hepburn sunglasses, but you do have to **spy on someone** (without putting yourself in danger). Follow somebody in your neighborhood or office complex; eavesdrop on a conversation on the bus; listen in on someone else's obnoxious cell phone conversation. When you can list *five things* about this person other than outward appearances, you have completed this exercise. (Examples: name, cell phone number, destination, spouse's name, any disease or ailment, name of client, etc.)

34 Because I want to be prepared for anything

Lions and tigers and earthquakes and terrorists and hurricanes and gas leaks and broken mains ... Oh my! Boy Scouts aren't the only ones who need to be prepared. Choose the *disaster du jour* and prepare for it with these activities.

Complete at least four activities below:

❑ Do you know where the **main turn-off valves**/knobs are for gas and water in your home? Locate them. If they require a wrench to close them, store a wrench nearby. Test to see that you are strong enough to operate them and show them to all people living in your home, including housesitters and babysitters.

❑ Do you have a **first-aid kit** in your home? Do you know how to use it? Assemble/buy one and review its use. Include easy-to-follow instructions.

❑ How do you get help? What phone number do you call in case of **emergency**? Do you have your address posted near your telephone at home and in the office? Do you have a panic button on your home alarm system? When and how should you use it? What do you dial from your cell phone if you witness an accident? Do your children know the procedures in case you're incapacitated? Make sure you can answer "yes" to all these questions.

❑ Don't carry a cell phone? Put one in your car anyway. In the US, cell phones are regulated by the FCC and must be able to dial 911, even if they are not hooked up to a service. Get hold of a **used cell phone** (buy it at a yard sale, take your teen's discarded model) and a cigarette lighter power adaptor (so you don't have to worry about a charge). You can also buy simple phones for around $10 at a cell phone shop, but insist that you want it without service, or check your church or local VOA for free phone programs. Store the phone and phone adaptor under your car seat for emergencies (not in the glove box where things get stolen).

❑ Put together an **earthquake-preparedness** kit. Store it in an accessible place. You can get advice on how to put this together at your local fire department or on-line. In addition, you can purchase a kit on the Red Cross Web site (www.redcross.org). If you already have a kit in your home, rotate the food supplies and batteries and make sure it is still accessible to complete this activity. (Substitute a flood kit, a terrorist-attack kit or another disaster kit, depending on your situation.)

❑ Read about the activities of *three* disaster-stricken areas. Where do you feel the most need is? Make a **donation** to a relief organization helping in that area.

❑ Make or buy a **mobile survival kit** and store it in your automobile. Again, you can find advice for this on-line or at your AAA or fire department. If you already have a kit in your car, rotate the batteries and make sure everything is still useable to complete this activity.

❑ Does your family have an **escape route** in case of a house fire? Survival rates increase in homes with a plan. Do you need ladders? Do you have keys in/near double bolts? How will you escape through security bars? Where is your family meeting place? Plan an escape route to complete this activity. The Los Angeles Fire Department has excellent advice, no matter where you live, at www.neighborhoodpreparedness.info. Or, visit your local fire department for advice.

❑ Install **smoke detectors** in your home. If you already have smoke detectors installed, test them and rotate the batteries. Mark your calendar to check the batteries in spring and fall, on the day Daylight Savings Time switches over.

❑ Make a **post-disaster plan.** How would you and your family receive emergency news if power and cell service were cut in your area for a long period of time? How would you contact each other? Could you access funds? Do you have a battery-powered radio available? Do you have a third party, out of the area, where you can report in? Think through the 24, 48 and 72 hours after a disaster and make a plan with your family.

❑ If you are a runner, walker, biker or hiker, or just often find yourself alone without identification, purchase a **personal ID tag** listing emergency contacts and medical information (if necessary). Now – wear it!

❏ Secure your **vital documents.** This could mean renting a safe-deposit box or buying a fireproof home safe. Some experts say use both. Your home safe should have an Underwriters Laboratory rating to withstand intense heat for an hour (enough for a minor fire). Use this for anything you might need quickly, but could replace if your home burns to the ground or washes away in a flood. The safe-deposit box is for items you rarely need, such as titles, deeds, birth and death certificates, stocks, photo negatives or computer back-up materials.

❏ Put together a home **inventory** for insurance purposes and store it in a safe place, outside your home.

❏ Keep your **kids safe.** Teach them computer security procedures (no personal information; never meet someone you met on-line without your parents' knowledge; etc.); fill out an identification kit with fingerprints and updated photos in case of disappearance.

❏ Watch *three* **disaster movies**: Spencer Tracy in *San Francisco* about the 1906 earthquake, 1978's *Swarm* about killer bees, *Towering Inferno*, *Twister*, *Outbreak*! or the mother of them all – *Earthquake*. You won't have trouble finding a variety. What did you learn from these films – other than you don't like disaster flicks? Now compare what you "learned" with reality. Go to the Center for Disease Control Web site (www.bt.cdc.gov) and then search the site for the disease of your choice. Scroll through the search results and click on the choice "What we learn about ___ threats from movies – fact or fiction?" (If you don't have access to the Internet, you can check the facts at your local library.)

❏ Prepare your **will** and arrange an executor for your estate.

❏ Prepare an **advance health care directive** (AHCD). An AHCD is a document that instructs others about your care should you be unable to make decisions on your own.

❏ Write an **ethical will.** Ethical wills assume that we are all more than the sum of our material parts and that we should try to pass along intangibles. They are letters or documents, usually addressed to grown children, recounting family history and expressing hope that the writer will be remembered for certain values. What values do you want to leave behind? Put them on paper (or video or DVD) and enclose them with your will.

Kathy: *"I really like that this experience makes you try a few new things – not too many, but enough to get you a little outside your comfort-zone and do things you might not otherwise do. I probably would not have gone to another religion's services without having Excuse #21 (because I need a little peace and spirituality) as a reason."*

35 Because I want to see the back of my closet

"He who knows he has enough is rich." Lao Tzu

Lao Tzu obviously never hit a shoe sale at Filene's Basement. Or shopped for coffee filters at Costco. He probably doesn't have a stack of last year's Lands' End catalogs in his bathroom, either. Many of us not only know we have enough, we know we have too much – and we'd like to get rid of some of it! But often the big clutter picture is just too overwhelming to tackle. These activities let you develop a taste for de-cluttering with some smaller jobs that will, nonetheless, make a big difference.

Complete at least five activities from the list below:

❑　Toss all **magazines** more than six months old. If you haven't read it yet, you probably won't. Back issues can almost always be found on-line or at the local library. The easiest solution is to recycle them. Do not fall into the *"I-want-to-donate-them-to-a-senior-center-but-I-haven't-had-the-time"* trap. You'll never have the time. Get the magazines out of your house now and make a plan to drop back issues off at a senior center each month in the future (those that accept magazines want newer issues, any way).

❑　Sell something on **eBay** (www.ebay.com). First take a tour around the Web site and see what kinds of things other people are selling. First time there? You'll be amazed! Everything from old toys to clothing to tractors is for sale. Now post your own ad to sell something around your house. (Be sure to read the instructions in the "Sell" area before proceeding.) Be careful. This can be both lucrative and addictive!

❑　**Make art** out of clutter. Do you have matchboxes/string/rubber bands/coupons/magazines/concert tickets/check stubs/department store bags/single socks that are cluttering up your drawers, bulletin boards or closets? Make art from them! Arrange and frame your matchboxes. Collage your shopping bags or magazines. Make a soft sculpture of your mate-less socks. Then, either display it or throw it away, but DO NOT store it in a closet or drawer!

❑ Line up all your **shoes**. Dig them out of every closet and put them end-to-end in front of you (you may want to do this when your spouse isn't home). Now make four signs and put them around the room: TOSS. FIX. SELL. KEEP. Try on the first pair and ask yourself the following questions. (A "yes" answer to any of these questions sends them to the designated pile.)

- Are these shoes worn out? Throw them in the TOSS pile.

- Do these shoes need any maintenance – polishing, new soles, new shoelaces? Throw them in the FIX pile.

- Will these shoes cause me pain – blisters, sprained ankle? Depending on their condition, throw them in the TOSS or SELL pile.

- Do I look stupid trying to walk in these shoes? Again, TOSS or SELL.

- Did I buy these shoes because of the price/style/cute shoe salesman but I've never, ever worn them? TOSS or SELL!

- Do these shoes smell bad? TOSS or FIX them!

- Is this shoe missing its mate? TOSS it!

- Are these shoes pitifully out of style? TOSS them!

- Do I hate these shoes? TOSS or SELL!

- Do I wear these shoes? KEEP!

- Now, either toss, sell, fix or keep your shoes, depending on your decision. Do this exercise twice, at least one month apart, to count this activity.

❑ Practice the "**one-in, one-out**" rule for the duration of the course. If you bring in one magazine, you must recycle one magazine. If you bring in one new book, you must get rid of one book (this is easy if you use the library!). If you buy one new pair of jeans, you must get rid of one pair of jeans. These items can be donated to charity, sold, thrown away, offered to friends – but they MUST leave your home!

❑   **Opt-out** of mailbox clutter. If you seem to be on everybody's mailing list, just get off! The Direct Marketing Association's Mail Preference service lets you "opt-out" of receiving direct mail marketing from national companies registered with the DMA. The listing lasts for five years. They also have an email preference service that lasts two years. Complete this activity by opting out of both services:

Opt-out of mail:
Direct Marketing Association
Mail Preference Service
PO Box 643
Carmel, NY 10512
(Or, print form or register on-line at:
www.the-dma.org/consumers/offmailinglist.html)

Opt-out of email: www.dmaconsumers.org/offemaillist.html

❑   Retire the **expired.** Allow yourself 60 minutes for each step in this activity. Do *two* of the following:

• Rx for your medicine cabinet. Clean out your medicine cabinet, discarding all obsolete and unused prescriptions, over-the-counter drugs, ointments and creams after checking the expiration dates. How do you discard them? The US EPA has deemed flushing expired medications down the toilet as "the least desirable way to dispose of any drug" because not all the medications are broken down in the water management treatment process ... (you thought this would be easy, didn't you?) Alternatives include returning the items to your pharmacy for incineration or, at the advice of some household hazardous waste facilities, you can render the medications unusable by putting glue (such as Elmer's) in with the pills and throwing them out in a sealed container. Check with your local pharmacist for the best solution. Some communities also have a hazardous waste collection site/day set aside. Be sensible in terms of quantity when you replace expired items and, of course, if you have children living in or visiting your house, make sure that all medications are in a child-proof location, including those you discard.

- Paper cutter: If you are a coupon clipper, toss out all expired coupons. In addition, recycle all old mail order catalogs, restaurant and shopping guides, calendars and phone books.

- Sort through your make-up. Anything that is cracked or dried up gets tossed. Any mascara over four months old is out. Anything with a case that no longer closes (so it cannot keep out bacteria) should be trashed. And anything that you don't remember buying is probably past its best-if-used-by date. Don't forget to replace old make-up brushes, as well. Keep only the make-up that you use. Organize in a clean, attractive and accessible fashion.

- Spread a little sunshine. Sunscreens can deteriorate over time. Throw out any expired bottles and tubes. In addition, if you don't see an expiration date, but the product seems to have dried up or changed consistency, toss it. (And if your sunscreen label is in Turkish, but you last visited Turkey in 1987, chances are, it's deteriorated.) The dollars you save aren't worth the damage to your family's skin. Replace only what you think you'll use.

❏ A few key clutter busters in your **kitchen** can work wonders. Complete *two* of the following:

- Gather your plastic food containers from around the house. Match each with a lid. Throw away anything without a matching lid, anything that's cracked or anything that doesn't have a strong seal. Some of the higher quality plastic wear lines, like Tupperware (www.tupperware.com), offer lifetime warranties or replacement parts. You may want to contact them. Replace only those pieces you will use. Organize them in an accessible manner.

- Sharpen your skills. Gather all your kitchen knives. Any with loose handles that cannot be fixed, throw away (in a safe place). Test the sharpness of your knives. Sharpen them (or take them to the nearest knife sharpener). A sharp knife is a safer knife.

- Count your coffee filters. Divide by the number of pots of coffee you prepare each day. How many days' (or years') worth do you have? The life expectancy of an American woman is currently 29,127 days. Keep only enough coffee filters for your lifespan. Donate or give away the rest to your friends. Do not buy any more.

- Allow yourself one hour. Empty your refrigerator. Wipe it out using the recommended cleaning solution for your model. If you have adjustable shelves, now is the time to adjust them to fit your lifestyle. Discard any expired items. Consolidate half-used jars of duplicate foods. If you have a box of baking soda in there for freshness, replace it. Throw away or use up those jars of strange foods bought for odd recipes. Now wipe the items clean as you put them back into the refrigerator. Replace only those items you will use.

❑ Organize your **sock drawer.** Keep mate-less socks in a lingerie bag and store for a season and then toss. Check each pair for holes and either mend or replace. (If you decide to mend them, you're not finished with this exercise until you've finished mending them and putting them away.) Throw out any pantyhose with runs or holes (even if you wear them under slacks). If you have socks you have not worn for over 12 months, throw them away or donate them. Replace only those socks you will use.

❑ Because nobody needs an excuse to **wear diamonds** (or CZ), organize your jewelry. Do *three* of the following (from organizational guru Julie Morgenstern, www.juliemorgenstern.com) to complete this exercise:

- Organize your jewelry by occasion, by sets or by color group.

- Compartmentalize your jewelry: in beautiful boxes on your dresser, in fabric-covered boxes in your drawers or in acrylic drawers and on necklace trees in your closet.

- Create a file of receipts and appraisals for expensive pieces.

- Stash your most expensive (or valuable) pieces in a jewelry safe or diversion safe (fake can of cleanser).

- Obtain and use protective travel pouches or portable jewelry cases for travel. (Morgenstern suggests stringing your necklaces through drinking straws!)

- Baby your baubles. Place ring bowls by your sinks, a small jewelry box by your computer and a velvet pouch in your handbag to catch jewelry you strip off during the day.

❑ For this next exercise you will need a small garbage can, a pencil sharpener and one hour of time. Go from room to room with both of these. In each room, find every **writing utensil** and test it. Toss any pens into the garbage can that are out of ink or cracked and threatening to leak. Any highlighters that are dried up? Into the garbage can. Throw away any chewed up pencils or those under two inches in length. Sharpen the rest. Don't forget to check your purse and briefcase! Now when you reach for a pen or pencil, it will work! Put a pad of paper by each phone, along with your writing utensils, and you're finished! No more excuses for missed messages!

36 Because I want to go digital

So you finally got that digital camera. Now what do you do with it? Even the most-experienced photographers are sometimes flummoxed by the technology in these little boxes. These activities are designed to get you over the technology and on to the fun and creativity.

Complete all seven exercises:

❑ Read the **instruction manual** for your digital camera. Yes, it sounds obvious, but have you really done it? The secret is to read PAST the two pages of "quick start" advice and TRY each feature as you read about it. (After you've read the instructions, you'll be shooting A LOT of photos, so you'll have plenty of chances to practice.)

❑ **Learn** how to do each of the following (if applicable to your camera):

- Load the batteries.

- Charge rechargeable batteries.

- Load/unload the memory stick/memory card.

- Turn camera on/off.

- Switch between still and movie modes.

- Turn LCD viewer on/off.

- Check last recorded image, both still and movie. Zoom in/out on that image.

- Zoom in/out when taking a photo.

- Use the macro (close-up) function.

- Take a timed photo – of yourself, preferably.

- Use different flash modes and levels (Twilight? Red-eye?).

- Delete a file from the camera (still and movie).

- Cancel an accidental deletion.

- Change the date/time/year. Turn this function on/off.

- Put an audio/text notation with your photo.

- Don't forget to read the troubleshooting section of your manual.

❑ Now it's time to discover your camera's **special features.** (Even your teenage kids might not know about these ... did they read the manual?) If your camera does any of the following, learn how to do it:

- Shoot photos using different effects: Solarize – the photo looks like an illustration. Black and White – the picture is monochrome. Sepia – the photo's colored like an old picture. Negative Art – the color and brightness are reversed.

- Save photos in different file sizes: small for emails; large for high-quality prints.

- Record files/photos in different file modes for different reasons. (TIFF? TEXT? VOICE? JPEG?)

- Adjust the record time for movie images.

- Protect an image from accidental deletion.

- Shoot photos using different flash levels. (No more washed-out head shots or dark photos!)

- Adjust the exposure. (Take your old SLR skills digital!)

- Change the language on your screen.

- Turn off the beep for those clandestine shots.

- Adjust the LCD brightness.

- Turn on special settings for twilight or landscape photography. (Be sure to test them!)

❑ Shoot **100 photos.** This is to help you change your mindset from a film camera. Digital photos are free. It's okay to take more than one shot of a subject to ensure that eyes are open and mouths are not. It's okay to shoot something just for the fun of it. Try some of the features you've learned about: Shoot a couple of architectural shots in black and white. Solarize your cat. Just shoot until you've reached 100 shots (you may have to move on to the next activity halfway through your shooting, depending on the memory capacity of your camera).

❑ Now that you've captured those photos in your camera, how do you get them out? Following the directions on your computer and/or camera, learn how to **download** your photos!

- Download your photos to a computer.

- Save your photos.

- Restart your computer and locate your saved photos.

- Delete the photos from your camera.

❑ First we had to sit through hours of Uncle Harry's slides of cousin Darlene's second birthday party. Then we had to sit through cousin Darlene's videos of her honeymoon in Hawaii. Now we have to crowd around Darlene's son's digital camera to see photos of Darlene's grandson's first steps displayed on the back of his super-tiny LCD screen! Your friends and relatives will thank you for this next activity. Complete at least *two* of the following (and promise never to show your vacation photos on a 2-inch screen – there are just too many BETTER ways to **share your photos!)**

- Print a photo at home using your computer or a digital photo printer.

- Save your photo onto a CD or floppy disk and print it in the photo department of a local store.

- Print a photo via an on-line photo center (Costco, Wal-Mart and Sam's Club all have on-line sites) and pick it up at the store (or have it mailed to you).

- Email a photo to a friend. (Check on the file sizes before attempting this. You can reduce the size of photos to email using your computer or some cameras.)

- Post a photo on a Web site.

- Make a screen saver using one of your photos.

- Share your photos via an on-line album (great for wedding or travel photos so you don't have to email them). See on-line photo centers such as www.snapfish.com and www.shutterfly.com.

- Make a slide show on your computer and show your family and friends. (Remember to edit your photos down to just your favorites.)

❑ Devise a **storage strategy** for your digital photo files. Don't be afraid to delete those photos you don't like. You may want to download photos and save them to CDs or DVDs each year for future reference. You can also buy on-line storage via some photo Web sites. If your computer has enough memory capacity, you may just want to keep them handy on your hard drive. With any system, make sure they are easily accessible via date or subject matter on the file "folders" and file names.

37 Because I really, really need to do this

There are things in life that we put off, and there are things in life that we *PUT OFF!* Things that we know we should learn to do or that we have never done because we're afraid or just can't focus. These are big things, so you're only required to achieve one of them. There's no excuse now that you have the support around you.

Complete one of the following:
(or confront your own "big issue")

❑ Learn to **swim**. Take an adult swimming course. Hire a hunky lifeguard for private lessons. Learn along with your three-year-old. Do whatever it takes. You should be able to jump feet first into the water and swim 100 yards without touching the side of the pool or standing on the bottom. You should also be able to float.

❑ Learn to drive a **stick shift**. Picture yourself speeding along in a red sports car, the roar of the engine … you should also be able to start on a hill and drive in traffic without crying to complete this activity.

❑ Learn **CPR**. Enroll in a course at work, through a community center or hospital. Complete the requirements and certification test.

❑ Get a mammogram and/or a pap smear. Have a dental **checkup**. Get your moles mapped at the dermatologist. If you have been putting off any of these medical tests/tasks because of fear (be honest), you can finish this activity by completing one of them.

❑ Hold a **snake**. This does not mean walk out into the desert and pick up a rattlesnake. This means that you finally say, "Enough is enough!" and enroll in a program designed to help you get over the fear. Your local zoo or hospital can help you find a reputable ophidiophobia or snakephobia program. Then, after you've completed the course – hold a snake.

❑ Fly in an **airplane**. One in eight Americans deliberately avoids commercial airline flights. If fear of flying (aviophobia or aerophobia) has been plaguing you, enroll in a reputable course and pledge to get over it. Then, take off to some place relaxing for a reward.

❑ Conquer a **weight issue.** If you are overweight, enroll in a reputable program and stick to it for the duration of this course. If you suffer from another sort of eating disorder, again, consult your physician and get help.

❑ Get **counseling.** Have you been saying that you really need counseling on an issue? Go and get it. Consult your physician's office, a local hotline, or a counseling referral service (often listed in your health plan) to find a reputable counselor.

❑ Go **back to school.** Take a tangible step towards making it happen: take the LSAT, GRE or similar test; meet with an admissions officer – in person; register for a class; apply for financial aid. Sending away for catalogs or checking out schools on-line are good first steps, but you must make a bigger commitment than that to complete this activity.

38 Because I need to exercise my brain

Even if you hate to exercise, these activities may be for you. How about a little "mental exercise?" (No, you're not going to sit on the couch thinking about doing sit-ups.) If you sometimes feel you're losing your mind, or at least your memory, these activities will introduce you to ways you can better remember names, lists and everyday information. The activities, exercises and outright tricks come from several areas – from experts in training, to organizations working with age-related fears about memory loss. Here's your excuse to sample some new techniques.

Complete at least four of these exercises:

❏ Here's a way to work on-going mental exercise into your routine – as well as your social life. **Commit to playing** a board or card game – backgammon, checkers, chess, cribbage, Mah Jongg, bridge are good ones – *once a week* during this course. The mental stimulation required to focus on the game (turn off the TV) and anticipate your opponent's next move provides mental stimulation (and exercise). Also, it's a nice alternative to another night in front of the TV.

❏ Take up crossword puzzles, jumbles or some other **word games**. Try Sudoko. Do *one every day for a week*, three times during the course. These types of games make you practice recalling information from your long-term memory, including infrequently used words. You can find these games in your local paper, but don't be intimidated if you can't complete *The New York Times* Sunday crossword in ink the first time! (They start out easy on Monday and get more difficult throughout the week.) You can also buy puzzle books, or check out www.m-w.com for Merriam Webster's free daily word games.

❏ The experts on Neurobics at the Department of Neurobiology in the Duke University Medical Center say you can **exercise your brain** by using your five physical senses and your emotional sense in unexpected ways – shaking up everyday routines. Do at least *three* of these exercises designed to stimulate your brain:

- Get dressed or take a shower with your eyes closed.

- Eat a meal with your family in silence. Use only visual cues.

- Listen to a specific piece of music while smelling a particular aroma.

- Go camping for the weekend.

- Take your child, spouse or parent to your workplace for the day.

- Take a completely new route to work.

- Shop at a farmer's market instead of a supermarket.

- Completely rearrange your office and desktop.

- Change the hand you normally write with for a few hours or an entire day.

- Draw or paint with your non-dominant hand.

❏ Read an **Op-Ed piece** in your local newspaper. Think about how this particular information is personally meaningful to you. Link the information to memories. This technique, called "Deep Processing," is one useful way to remember what you've read. Now discuss the article with someone. Did you remember more of the facts by relating them to yourself? Try this *four* times over the course.

❏ Students are taught that a good way to remember information when studying for a test is to "**talk it out.**" Try this technique before an upcoming meeting, interview or presentation. After you've read or studied something you will be expected to know, talk about it to yourself. Explain it, out loud. Pretend you are teaching a course in it. Do this with your office door closed, while driving to work, while you're doing dishes, while you're running. Make sure you do it OUT LOUD! Practice this technique *three* times in different situations to see if it works for you.

❏ Try this technique for learning **names**: Go to a party or function where you will be meeting a lot of new people. With each person you meet, associate his or her name with an image in your mind. For instance, picture Robert Green playing golf on the green, or with a green face. If you meet Teresa Martinez, think of Mother Teresa drinking martinis. Do this for each person you meet. The next day, make a list of the names of people you met the previous day. Did you remember more than usual?

❏ Memorize **a poem**. Recite it to an audience: your child, your lover or even at your next get-together!

❏ List every man you've ever **kissed**. That should get your memory in shape. (You may want to keep this list mental, instead of writing it down for your family to find!)

❑ Learning a **new language** exercises your brain in myriad ways (when it isn't frustrating it!). Tony Buzan, a memory expert (www.buzancentre.com), points out that just 100 words make up half of all conversation. For this exercise, learn the following 100 words in a language you have been trying to learn (or learned a long time ago).

A, an	After	Again	All
Almost	Also	Always	And
Because	Before	Big	But
I can	I come	Either/or	I find
First	For	Friend	From
I go	Good	Good-bye	Happy
I have	He	Hello	Here
How	I	I am	If
In	I know	Last	I like
Little	I love	I make	Many
One	More	Most	Much
My	New	No	Not
Now	Of	Often	On
One	Only	Or	Other
Our	Out	Over	People
Place	Please	Same	I see
She	So	Some	Sometimes
Still	Such	I tell	Thank you
That	The	Their	Them
Then	There is	They	Thing
I think	This	Time	To
Under	Up	Us	I use
Very	We	What	When
Where	Which	Who	Why
With	Yes	You	Your

❑ Try another memory technique. Read the following list of sports one time. When you are done, write down as many of the sports as you can remember without looking back at the list:

snow skiing	basketball	tennis
long jump	bobsledding	100-meter dash
hockey	baseball	ice skate
discus	golf	high jump
volleyball	javelin	soccer
luge	curling	cricket
decathlon	hurdles	

How many did you remember? Now you will practice a memory method promoted by the University of Texas at Austin Learning Center called "Grouping." Take another look at the list, but this time, group the sports into: "Winter Sports," "Track and Field Sports," and "Sports using a Ball." Now, cover the list again and see how many you remember. Did you remember more? Use this technique at least *four* times during the course, for grocery lists, errands, packing suitcases, schoolwork and, of course, remembering lists of sporting events.

❑ Commit to **focusing** your attention. By focusing on what you are trying to remember, experts say you can remember more of what you have read, studied, etc. In other words – cool the multi-tasking when you want something to sink in! (By the way, this is especially true as we age; so don't tell your teenagers to turn off the music while they're studying just yet!) Try one of these exercises to complete this activity:

- Are you in a book group? For the next book you are reading, read only when you can devote your attention to the book: no television on in the background, no radio talk show, no lunch-time conversation. See if you remember more and if the discussion is richer for you.

- Next time you are reading the newspaper or a magazine, give yourself some peace and turn off the radio or television. (Also, go easy on the martinis!) Do this for a week and see if you are more in-tune to the details of the news.

- For one week, make a point of turning on the television only for those programs you want to watch, instead of having constant background noise. See if you enjoy or retain more from the programs you do choose to watch. (If you want "company" try soothing music or human conversation.)

39 Because I love my pet

They take such good care of us; we should do the same for them. Consider this an excuse to pamper a special member of your household.

Complete four activities below:

❏ Read an "**owner's manual**" for your pet. This can be a simple guide to first-time pet ownership (probably aimed at children) or a full-fledged medical guide. You can also read three magazines aimed at owners of your type of pet to complete this activity.

❏ **Exercise** your pet. If you have a dog, walk it every day for a week – especially if it's penned up in the yard. If you already have a walking routine, step up the activity (appropriate to age and breed) every day for a week. If you have a cat, play with it at least 20 minutes a day for a week. Do you notice a difference in your pet? Are you both beginning to expect the playtime? Do this *four* times during the program.

❏ Get your **family involved** with your pet. Set up a rotation for any of the ongoing activities: brushing, feeding, cleaning the litter box, exercising. In order to complete this activity, adhere to the plan.

❏ Make sure all your pet's **vaccinations** are up to date. Take your pet in for a check-up. Discuss any special considerations (aging, breeding, fleas, travel) with your veterinarian.

❏ If you travel with your pet, or are expecting to move, have an **identity chip** inserted and register it with the appropriate agency.

❏ Make sure your pet has a well-fitting collar and **proper identification** tags.

❏ Revamp your **pet's pad**: replace worn-out supplies such as litter boxes, beds, houses, aquariums, etc.

❏ Buy your pet a **frivolous gift**: a new toy or collar or bubbling scuba diver for its aquarium.

❏ Teach your old pet a **new trick**.

❏ Check with your vet, your pet store or a pet magazine to make sure your **pet's diet** is appropriate to its age, living conditions, etc.

❏ Have a **portrait** made of your pet – a painting, drawing or a photograph. Or, make one yourself. Frame and display it with the family pictures.

❏ If you've been meaning to have your pet **spayed** or **neutered**, do it.

❏ Give your cat a ***pet*-icure**.

❏ **Brush** your pet *daily* for the duration of this course. You will see a notable decrease in hair around the house (unless, of course, you have a pet boa constrictor).

40 Because I need more than a makeover

Whether it's a house, a body or an outlook on life, television has given us an "extreme" range of ways to improve our face/house/buttocks/relationship/hair/child-rearing skills/nose/diet/cooking. Here's your excuse to take your fascination with these makeover programs one step further and adopt some of the advice.

Complete the first activity and at least four more:

❏ Start a style **identity file,** whether it's for your home or your wardrobe. At www.visual-therapy.com Visual Therapy image consulting firm suggests that you include fashion pictures from magazines, photos of people and places, swatches of fabric, buttons, ads, catalogue pages, etc. Use this file when you are completing any of the other exercises for this excuse.

❏ Make over your **make-up.** Visit at least three cosmetics counters for a new look. Be honest with the cosmetician and tell him/her that you are test-driving three before making a decision. Don't be tempted (or pressured) to take out a second mortgage for new eye shadow at the first counter. After your three trials, budget permitting, buy new supplies for a new you.

❏ Make over a **holiday.** Are you always disappointed that you're not carrying on a family tradition? Did a three-day weekend just go by without your remembering why you had the day off? Do you want your family to focus on the meaning of a holiday, rather than the payoff? For this activity, do something constructive to bring meaning or tradition back to a special day. If it's your own birthday, take your mom out to lunch. If it's someone else's – bake a cake and hand out party hats! On Memorial Day, attend a commemoration or place a wreath at the cemetery. Gather mom, grandma and the kids to bake Christmas cookies or cook a traditional Thanksgiving menu for friends. Remember to be realistic and, most of all, enjoy the day.

❏ Choose an area measuring approximately 2 square yards and make it over. This could be a balcony or corner of your garden (do this in tandem with *Excuse #26: Because I need to stop and smell the roses*); a play corner for your child; your desk (do this in addition to *Excuse #35: Because I want to see the back of my closet*); a reading nook; a window area; a guest bath; etc. By taking on a **small area**, you should be able to complete the makeover without feeling overwhelmed.

❏ Make over a piece of **furniture.** This could be re-caning an antique chair; painting a bookcase and organizing the books; waxing a dresser and lining the drawers with scented paper; making slip covers for an eyesore sofa; painting your garden furniture in wild colors; or, depending on how broad your definition of "furniture" is, even replacing that leaky toilet or cracked toilet seat. Have fun and be creative!

❏ Pay for the **advice** of a professional make-up artist, hair colorist, hair stylist or wardrobe consultant (or all four!). Take time to discuss what you want in a new look. Don't just say "Julia Roberts," bring in photos (front and back for hair) and think about what you want, how much time you're willing to spend, your budget, etc. Then – let them do their jobs!

❏ Make over your **bed.** Does your mattress need replacing – or even just flipping? Are you using the right pillow for your sleep habits? Is your comforter the right weight for the temperature of your room? Do you like the way your bed looks? What's hidden underneath? This is your excuse to make your dreams come true – or at least more comfortable. Replace anything worn out or outdated and splurge on a new look. If cost is an issue, don't forget to look in your own linen closet for sheets and pillowcases and even grandma's quilt that you've been storing (and ignoring) for years.

❏ Let your girlfriend (or boyfriend) make you over. Do you have a friend (or relative) you're always ignoring who says, "That would look great on you!" **Give yourself over** to him/her for a day. See how other people see you. You might like what they see! (You can set some parameters – no haircuts, no tattoo removal, etc. if you'd like.)

❏ Visit a **makeover studio.** Usually you will not be receiving sensible, everyday advice – these studios specialize in sensuous and sexy looks with a professional stylist. Most offer a photo session at the end. (Remember those "boudoir shots" of the 80s?) Share the photo at the next get-together – if you dare!

❏ Raid your **sister's closet** one more time. Do you have a sister (or friend) who's about your size? Make a trade – permanent or not – and double your wardrobes. You wear her clothes; she wears yours. You can do this for a day, a weekend, or whatever you decide.

❏ Be an accessory to a makeover – or at least use **accessories.** With this activity, it's the little things that count. Solely by the use of accessories, make over a room, a sofa or an outfit of clothing. Throw pillows, candles, plants, jewelry, scarves, hats, belts – these are your tools. For your home – steal a picture from the living room to hang in the entryway; for your closet, pair your favorite jeans with a new sexy belt. Be creative and crack open that seldom-used jewelry box!

❏ Make over your **diet.** Consult a nutritionist. Usually she will want a food diary, your vital stats, results from a cholesterol test, etc. Find out how to cut down on fast food or plan better for meals – some will even come to your home to critique your kitchen shelves! Then, put the advice to work!

❏ **Quickie** makeovers. Do *three* of the following:

- Rearrange the furniture in one room.

- Pair two items in your closet that you've never worn together and wear them.

- Change one item in your diet to organic for the duration of this program.

- Get up half an hour earlier for a week. What do you do with the time?

- Go to bed half an hour earlier for two weeks. How do you feel?

- Wear the underwear at the bottom of your underwear drawer (hopefully, it's really sexy) instead of the stuff you always wear.

- Dress up when you go some place where you usually grunge out – heels to the PTA meeting; shopping in a skirt or make-up to the gym!

- Go to a store and try on one outfit that you normally wouldn't – show some cleavage (or don't) for a change!

- Wear your hair up/down (but different) for a day.

❏ Make over **one meal** – for you, your kids, your partner or the whole family. This can focus on nutrition, cost, preparation time, calories, sit-down family time – whatever will improve that meal. There's plenty of help on-line (especially for kids' lunches). Taking a close look at one meal a day will kick-start other good habits. Continue these good habits for the duration of this program.

❏ Make over your repertoire of **tricks**. Not that you're an old dog, but for this activity, learn one new thing – from reading palms to scuba diving to sending attachments with your emails! This is your excuse to make yourself do something you've always wanted to! Have fun!

❏ Complete a **virtual makeover.** You'll need a digital photo and Internet access. Go to www.ivillage.co.uk. You have to download a software program, but the site allows you to try out different hairstyles, makeup, glasses and even eye colors. Put a few different looks together, print them out and show them at the next get-together.

What's your excuse?

Use the following pages to keep track of the excuses you want to make!
Use them to jot down notes, observations, plans, ideas or anything else
that will help you complete – and enjoy – the activities.

Excuse #____

Because _____

Notes:

Excuse #____

Because _____

Notes:

Excuse #____

Because _____

Notes:

Excuse #____

Because _____

Notes:

Excuse #____

Because _____

Notes:

Acknowledgements

My husband, Chris, who not only sparked the idea for this book, but survived the testing of most of the excuses!

Noel Weimer, Tina Gerritsen, Connie Moser, Lynn Woodside and Monika Bokma-Kackovic: Five creative, artistic and inspiring American women living in Amsterdam who never once let me make excuses and give up on writing this book.

Barbara Gazley, who designed a book that makes me hope it's "judged by the cover."

Kathy Keating, who argued over every comma and hyphen with me. (If there are any grammatical mistakes in these pages, it simply means I won the argument!)

About the Author

Nanci Tangeman has had lots of excuses to reinvent her life while moving around the world with her husband, Chris Blumenthal. Journalist, copywriter, consultant and humorist, each country – the United States, England, Uzbekistan and the Netherlands – brings new opportunities for work and adventure. Nanci was born in Burien, Washington and lives in Amsterdam (for now).

www.nancitangeman.com

894452

Made in the USA